I0894313

Table of Contents

Success Strategies

This section contains a list of test-taking strategies that you may find helpful as you work through the test. By taking what you know and applying logical thought, you can maximize your chances of answering any question correctly!

It is very important to realize that every question is different and every person is different: no single strategy will work on every question, and no single strategy will work for every person. That's why we've included all of them here, so you can try them out and determine which ones work best for different types of questions and which ones work best for you.

Question Strategies

Read Carefully

Read the question and answer choices carefully. Don't miss the question because you misread the terms. You have plenty of time to read each question thoroughly and make sure you understand what is being asked. Yet a happy medium must be attained, so don't waste too much time. You must read carefully, but efficiently.

Contextual Clues

Look for contextual clues. If the question includes a word you are not familiar with, look at the immediate context for some indication of what the word might mean. Contextual clues can often give you all the information you need to decipher the meaning of an unfamiliar word. Even if you can't determine the meaning, you may be able to narrow down the possibilities enough to make a solid guess at the answer to the question.

Prefixes

If you're having trouble with a word in the question or answer choices, try dissecting it. Take advantage of every clue that the word might include. Prefixes and suffixes can be a huge help. Usually they allow you to determine a basic meaning. Pre- means before, post- means after, pro - is positive, de- is negative. From prefixes and suffixes, you can get an idea of the general meaning of the word and try to put it into context.

Hedge Words

Watch out for critical hedge words, such as *likely, may, can, often, almost, mostly, usually, generally, rarely,* and *sometimes.* Question writers insert these hedge phrases to cover every possibility. Often an answer choice will be wrong simply because it leaves no room for exception. Be on guard for answer choices that have definitive words such as *exactly* and *always.*

Switchback Words

Stay alert for *switchbacks.* These are the words and phrases frequently used to alert you to shifts in thought. The most common switchback words are *but, although,* and *however.* Others include *nevertheless, on the other hand, even though, while, in spite of, despite, regardless of.* Switchback words are important to catch because they can change the direction of the question or an answer choice.

Face Value

When in doubt, use common sense. Accept the situation in the problem at face value. Don't read too much into it. These problems will not require you to make wild assumptions. If you have to go beyond creativity and warp time or space in order to have an answer choice fit the question, then you should move on and consider the other answer choices. These are normal problems rooted in reality. The applicable relationship or explanation may not be readily apparent, but it is there for you to figure out. Use your common sense to interpret anything that isn't clear.

Answer Choice Strategies

Answer Selection

The most thorough way to pick an answer choice is to identify and eliminate wrong answers until only one is left, then confirm it is the correct answer. Sometimes an answer choice may immediately seem right, but be careful. The test writers will usually put more than one reasonable answer choice on each question, so take a second to read all of them and make sure that the other choices are not equally obvious. As long as you have time left, it is better to read every answer choice than to pick the first one that looks right without checking the others.

Answer Choice Families

An answer choice family consists of two (in rare cases, three) answer choices that are very similar in construction and cannot all be true at the same time. If you see two answer choices that are direct opposites or parallels, one of them is usually the correct answer. For instance, if one answer choice says that quantity *x* increases and another either says that quantity *x* decreases (opposite) or says that quantity *y* increases (parallel), then those answer choices would fall into the same family. An answer choice that doesn't match the construction of the answer choice family is more likely to be incorrect. Most questions will not have answer choice families, but when they do appear, you should be prepared to recognize them.

Eliminate Answers

Eliminate answer choices as soon as you realize they are wrong, but make sure you consider all possibilities. If you are eliminating answer choices and realize that the last one you are left with is also wrong, don't panic. Start over and consider each choice again. There may be something you missed the first time that you will realize on the second pass.

Avoid Fact Traps

Don't be distracted by an answer choice that is factually true but doesn't answer the question. You are looking for the choice that answers the question. Stay focused on what the question is asking for so you don't accidentally pick an answer that is true but incorrect. Always go back to the question and make sure the answer choice you've selected actually answers the question and is not merely a true statement.

Extreme Statements

In general, you should avoid answers that put forth extreme actions as standard practice or proclaim controversial ideas as established fact. An answer choice that states the "process should be used in certain situations, if…" is much more likely to be correct than one that states the "process should be discontinued completely." The first is a calm rational statement and doesn't even make a definitive, uncompromising stance, using a hedge word *if* to provide wiggle room, whereas the second choice is a radical idea and far more extreme.

Benchmark

As you read through the answer choices and you come across one that seems to answer the question well, mentally select that answer choice. This is not your final answer, but it's the one that will help you evaluate the other answer choices. The one that you selected is your benchmark or standard for judging each of the other answer choices. Every other answer choice must be compared to your benchmark. That choice is correct until proven otherwise by another answer choice beating it. If you find a better answer, then that one becomes your new benchmark. Once you've decided that no other choice answers the question as well as your benchmark, you have your final answer.

Predict the Answer

Before you even start looking at the answer choices, it is often best to try to predict the answer. When you come up with the answer on your own, it is easier to avoid distractions and traps because you will know exactly what to look for. The right answer choice is unlikely to be word-for-word what you came up with, but it should be a close match. Even if you are confident that you have the right answer, you should still take the time to read each option before moving on.

General Strategies

Tough Questions

If you are stumped on a problem or it appears too hard or too difficult, don't waste time. Move on! Remember though, if you can quickly check for obviously incorrect answer choices, your chances of guessing correctly are greatly improved. Before you completely give up, at least try to knock out a couple of possible answers. Eliminate what you can and then guess at the remaining answer choices before moving on.

Check Your Work

Since you will probably not know every term listed and the answer to every question, it is important that you get credit for the ones that you do know. Don't miss any questions through careless mistakes. If at all possible, try to take a second to look back over your answer selection and make sure you've selected the correct answer choice and haven't made a costly careless mistake (such as marking an answer choice that you didn't mean to mark). This quick double check should more than pay for itself in caught mistakes for the time it costs.

Pace Yourself

It's easy to be overwhelmed when you're looking at a page full of questions; your mind is confused and full of random thoughts, and the clock is ticking down faster than you would like. Calm down and maintain the pace that you have set for yourself. Especially as you get down to the last few minutes of the test, don't let the small numbers on the clock make you panic. As long as you are on track by monitoring your pace, you are guaranteed to have time for each question.

Don't Rush

It is very easy to make errors when you are in a hurry. Maintaining a fast pace in answering questions is pointless if it makes you miss questions that you would have gotten right otherwise. Test writers like to include distracting information and wrong answers that seem right. Taking a little extra time to avoid careless mistakes can make all the difference in your test score. Find a pace that allows you to be confident in the answers that you select.

Keep Moving

Panicking will not help you pass the test, so do your best to stay calm and keep moving. Taking deep breaths and going through the answer elimination steps you practiced can help to break through a stress barrier and keep your pace.

Final Notes

The combination of a solid foundation of content knowledge and the confidence that comes from practicing your plan for applying that knowledge is the key to maximizing your performance on test day. As your foundation of content knowledge is built up and strengthened, you'll find that the strategies included in this chapter become more and more effective in helping you quickly sift through the distractions and traps of the test to isolate the correct answer.

Now it's time to move on to the test content chapters of this book, but be sure to keep your goal in mind. As you read, think about how you will be able to apply this information on the test. If you've already seen sample questions for the test and you have an idea of the question format and style, try to come up with questions of your own that you can answer based on what you're reading. This will give you valuable practice applying your knowledge in the same ways you can expect to on test day.

Good luck and good studying!

Reading: Literature

Living on a Ranch

Marcus Morgan lives in Laramie, Wyoming, with his family. Laramie is between the Snowy Mountain Range and the Laramie Mountain Range, west of Cheyenne, Wyoming.

Marcus and his family own a large cattle ranch outside of the city along U.S. Route 287. The Bar M Bar Ranch raises both beef and dairy cattle, along with a small herd of sheep. Mrs. Morgan keeps chickens and raises a small garden to feed the family. Marcus and his two brothers, James and Robert, have to help with chores and taking care of the animals.

Life starts early on the ranch. Mrs. Morgan rings the bell to bring everyone in for breakfast at 4:30 am. The family eats breakfast with the ranch hands, and then the boys do their morning chores before heading off to school. When the boys return from school, they have more chores to complete before dinner and time for homework.

Everyone has a job on a ranch. Mr. Morgan supervises the ranch hands, oversees repairs, and takes care of all the vehicles on the ranch. Mrs. Morgan is in charge of paying the bills and making sure everyone is fed. Marcus, at 15 years old, is the oldest child and has the most responsibility.

He has to let the sheep out every morning and bring them back in every evening. He helps in the milking barn or with branding beef cattle when needed. He also takes care of the working dogs used all over the ranch. James gathers eggs, brings in a fresh pail of milk every morning, and cleans out horse stalls in the evenings. Robert, the baby of the family, helps his mom around the house and in the garden.

Marcus especially likes working with the sheep. In the mornings, he and his favorite working dog, Shep, run the sheep out of their corral into the big pasture so they can graze. Marcus uses whistles and calls to tell Shep where he wants the sheep to go, and Shep herds them. In the evenings, Marcus and Shep round up the sheep from the pasture and return them to the corral. Then Marcus must feed the sheep and check them all for injuries. In the spring, Marcus and Shep help Mr. Morgan bring the sheep into the shearing shed one at a time to have their wool sheared.

1. Where is the Bar M Bar Ranch?
    a. Cheyenne, Wyoming
    b. The Snowy Mountains
    c. Laramie, Wyoming
    d. The Laramie Mountains

2. How does Marcus tell Shep what to do?
    a. Marcus uses a clicker in his hand.
    b. Marcus uses a leash.
    c. Marcus lets Shep do all the work alone.
    d. Marcus uses whistles and calls.

3. Which of the following choices best summarizes the fifth paragraph?
    a. Marcus and Shep take care of the sheep.
    b. Marcus enjoys working with the sheep.
    c. Shep is a good sheep dog.
    d. Mr. Morgan sheers the sheep in the spring.

4. From this passage, you can tell that:
    a. Everyone has a job on a ranch.
    b. Children work much harder than adults on the ranch.
    c. Living on a ranch is no fun.
    d. Marcus does not enjoy his chores.

5. Mr. Morgan supervises the ranch hands and the outside chores. Which of the following choices best describes Mrs. Morgan's chores?
    a. She is in charge of the sheep.
    b. She is in charge of the chickens.
    c. She is in charge of the household and bills.
    d. She is in charge of the children.

6. From the passage, the reader can tell:
    a. Ten ranch hands work on the Bar M Bar Ranch.
    b. Working and living on a ranch is a full time job.
    c. A ranch in Wyoming is a lonely place.
    d. Mr. Morgan doesn't like sheep.

7. From this passage, the phrase "ranch hands" most likely means:
    a. The hands of people who work on the ranch.
    b. People who work on a ranch owned by someone else.
    c. The machines used to milk dairy cattle.
    d. A way to repair a fence.

8. Marcus, James, and Robert are different ages, but they have something in common in this passage. Which sentence best describes what they have in common?
    a. They all help with chores on the ranch.
    b. They all take care of the working dogs.
    c. They all have brown hair.
    d. They all have to shear sheep.

Geocaching

"Would you like to go geocaching with me this weekend, Tommy?" asked his father. "I have found a couple of new ones near the creek that I think would be fun. We could invite your friend Sam to join us."

"Sure, Dad. I love geocaching," said Tommy. "Should we go Saturday?" They agreed that they would leave Saturday morning to find the new geocaches, and Tommy ran to call Sam and invite him. Sam agreed to come with them. Although he wasn't sure what geocaching was, he always had fun with Tommy and his dad.

Friday night, Tommy and his dad got their gear ready. Both of them had handheld GPS units, hiking boots with good wool socks, a backpack to carry first aid gear, water, and swag for the cache such as plastic soldiers, a water pistol, and some playing cards. Tommy's father made sure that they had a compass and a map, bug spray, and hats, and he printed out the coordinates for the geocaches. Tommy had given Sam a list of things to bring with him, as well.

Saturday morning, Tommy and Dad picked up Sam at his house and off they went. "Mr. Jones, could you explain to me what geocaching is?" Sam asked, as they were getting in the car.

"Of course, Sam. Basically, it's like a giant worldwide treasure hunt. People hide geocaches, or containers, then take the coordinates with their GPS and enter the coordinates into a website where people like us can find them. Then other people, like us, go hunting for these containers. Some of them are very tiny, just big enough to have a piece of paper for the date and your name. Some of them are large enough to hold books or toys and a logbook. Sometimes, people even put disposable cameras in them so you can take a picture of yourself at the cache. Sometimes, there are even items in the cache that can be tracked, so you can see how they move around the world."

Tommy's dad could see that Sam was still a little confused, but he knew that the boy would catch on as they got going. Mr. Jones put the coordinates for the first cache into his GPS, and off they went. "It looks like this first cache is only two miles from here," he told the boys.

The GPS led the trio to a small parking area just inside the local park, where they stopped and got their backpacks on, sprayed themselves with bug spray, and reset the GPS for off-road walking. "It looks like we have about 400 feet to go just that way," Mr. Jones said, as they headed away from the car into the woods. When they arrived at the location, Sam looked around. "I don't see anything," he complained.

Tommy laughed. "Our GPS is accurate to 15 feet, Sam, which means that the cache container is within 15 feet of Dad right now, but in any direction. The way we do it is Dad stands still, and I walk 15 feet from him. Then we know how far in each direction to look. Why don't I walk 15 feet to his right and you go left? Then we know exactly where to search." Sam agreed, and the boys quickly marked off their search area. "The cache is medium sized, Sam, so be looking for something like the plastic boxes your mom puts leftovers in, okay?"

Tommy, Sam, and Mr. Jones searched for about 10 minutes. They looked in tree branches, under rocks and leaves, and even inside of a hollow log before Sam yelled, "I think I found it!" Sure enough, he had found the container under a pile of leaves beside the hollow log. Since this was Sam's first find, Tommy and his dad let Sam open the box and choose an item to trade. Sam chose to take a bouncy rubber ball and leave a water gun. Mr. Jones signed the logbook for all of them, and they hid the cache back where they found it.

"That was so much fun, Tommy! I'm so glad you asked me to come along," Sam said excitedly.

"Does that mean you boys are ready to find the next one?" Mr. Jones asked. The boys cheered and the three set off for the car.

1. Why did Sam go with Tommy and Mr. Jones?
    a. He loved geocaching.
    b. Tommy offered to give him a water pistol.
    c. He always had fun when he was with Tommy and Mr. Jones.
    d. He wanted to go swimming in the creek.

2. Why did Sam and Tommy have to mark off a search area?
    a. The GPS was accurate only to 15 feet.
    b. Tommy's dad wanted to make the boys work harder.
    c. Searching a big area was more fun.
    d. Tommy wanted Sam to learn how to search.

3. Tommy gave Sam a list of items to bring with him. What might have been on that list?
    a. A towel, a beach ball, and a sand bucket
    b. A raincoat, an umbrella, and rubber boots
    c. Wool socks, hiking boots, and a backpack
    d. Books, a flashlight, and a tent

4. Which of the following sentences is the best summary of paragraph five?
    a. Geocaching is a treasure hunt for small containers using GPS coordinates.
    b. Geocaching is a game for people to play online.
    c. Geocaching is about logbooks and taking pictures.
    d. Geocaching is something only boys do.

5. From the passage, "swag" most likely means
   a. How a person walks
   b. Small items or toys to trade
   c. A bag with money in it
   d. A backpack to carry your gear in

6. In the car, Mr. Jones teaches Sam about geocaching. Does Tommy teach Sam anything?
   a. Yes, Tommy teaches Sam about using a backpack.
   b. No, Sam teaches Tommy about comic books.
   c. No, Mr. Jones teaches Sam about drawing on a map.
   d. Yes, Tommy teaches Sam about marking off a search area.

7. This story is about:
   a. Two friends going into the woods for an adventure
   b. Two friends going geocaching with Mr. Jones
   c. Tommy teaching Sam about searching
   d. Sam learning how to use a GPS

8. From clues in the story, "cache" most likely means:
   a. A hollow log
   b. A path through the woods
   c. A pirate's treasure
   d. A hiding place

Dance Class

Jillian and Samantha attend dance classes at Ms. Suzie's Dance Studio every Friday after school. The twins have matching leotards and tights. They both wear their long brown hair up in a bun. However, that's all they have in common at Ms. Suzie's.

Jillian loves classical dance and is taking a ballet class. After she went into the classroom, she put on her satin slippers and began to stretch her legs at the *barre*. Jillian watches herself in the wall-length mirrors to make sure her feet are moving correctly on the wooden floor. When Ms. Suzie turns on the music, Jillian and the other ballerinas get into line and settle into position one. Jillian stood with the balls of her feet completely turned out, her heels touching and her feet forming a straight line. As Ms. Suzie took the class through the other four positions, Jillian thought about what was coming up later. Ms. Suzie had promised that today they would start learning *en pointe*. "*En pointe*" is French for "on the tip," when ballerinas stand on the tip of their toes as they dance. Jillian brought special toe shoes with her today, reinforced to support her feet and protect her toes.

In another classroom, Samantha slipped into her tap shoes and began to warm up on the wooden floor. Tap shoes are like dress shoes with little metal plates under the toes and the heels. The plates are attached by small screws that can be loosened to change the sound of the tapping. Ms. Jessica, one of Ms. Suzie's dance instructors, started the music. Samantha and her friends started working on their tap steps, watching themselves in the mirrors on the wall. Samantha started with basic tap steps, called single steps, and quickly moved through the different steps like the brush, the shuffle, and the ball change. Samantha likes the modern movements and music of tap. Jillian and Samantha both are practicing with extra effort. The school recital is next week, and they want to do their very best. The recital was so important to them that last month, their dad built a mini dance studio in the basement. It has a wooden floor, mirrors, and a *barre*. There is only room enough for one of them to practice at a time, so they take turns in the mini studio. Jillian practices in the mornings and Samantha in the evenings. They are really ready for the big night.

After class, the girls walked home together excitedly talking about their classes.

1. Why do Jillian and Samantha go to Ms. Suzie's?
    a. They want to learn to dance.
    b. They want to learn how to dress alike.
    c. Jillian talked Samantha into taking a ballet class.
    d. They just pass by on their way home.

2. Although they are dressed alike, the girls are very different. What is the big difference between them?
    a. Jillian has blonde hair, while Samantha's is brown.
    b. Samantha is wearing shorts, but Jillian is wearing a leotard.
    c. Jillian loves ballet, and Samantha loves tap.
    d. Samantha walks home, and Jillian takes the bus.

3. Ms. Suzie and Ms. Jessica both teach dance classes in studios. What did the two classrooms have in common?

a. Both classrooms have TV's and game machines in them.
b. Both classrooms have shoe cubbies and rugs.
c. Both classrooms have wood walls and carpets.
d. Both classrooms have wooden floors and mirrors.

4. According to the passage, ballet is:

a. Only for girls
b. Only for boys
c. A classical type of dance
d. A modern type of dance

5. A "*barre*" is:

a. A bar of soap in the dish
b. A bar of light through a window
c. A bar of chocolate to eat after class
d. A bar on the wall for stretching

6. This story mostly is about:

a. After school programs for boys
b. How much the sisters loved dance
c. Friends having fun together
d. How much the dad loves the twins

Island Ponies

Assateague Island is on the east coast. It is a long, thin island. It is so long that two-thirds of it is in Maryland and one-third in Virginia. The Maryland end of the island has most of the Assateague National Seashore and Assateague Park. The southern end of the island, in Virginia, has the Chincoteague National Wildlife Refuge.

Two herds of wild ponies live on this island. The ponies that live in Maryland are called the Assateague horses, and the ponies that live in Virginia are called the Chincoteague ponies. Standing only an average of 13.2 hands high, or 54 inches, they are considered ponies because of how short they are. Both herds look alike, too. The ponies can be either solid colored or pinto patterned. The two herds are the same kind of horses, but they are treated very differently.

The Assateague horses are considered wild animals. Unless there is a dire need, they are left alone to survive on the poor habitat available on the Assateague National Seashore. The rangers do not give them vet checkups, or teach them to ride or even like being around humans. They live as they have since the first ponies came to the island after a Spanish galleon sank off the coast in the 1500's.

A vet, however, checks the Chincoteague ponies twice a year. They are given shots and kept healthy, despite the poor vegetation on the island. The Virginia ponies are used to people because of this treatment. The Chincoteague herd is managed by the Chincoteague Volunteer Fire Department, which holds a very special pony sale every year.

Assateague Island isn't very big, so the herds have to be kept small so they all have enough food and room. Both herds average 150 ponies. To keep the herd that small, every year in July the Fire Department rounds up the Chincoteague ponies by using bigger horses to drive them into the water for the 10 minute swim to Chincoteague Island. The ponies are checked by vets, and then some of them are sold to spectators who want a pony of their very own. The remainder of the herd is allowed to rest, and then they are pushed to swim back to their home island.

The money from this sale helps the Fire Department buy new equipment and pays for the veterinarians who take care of the herd. It also helps to keep people interested in the ponies. So many people come to this sale and love the ponies that there was even a famous children's book written about one of the first ponies sold.

1. Which sentence best summarizes paragraph 2?
    a. Assateague horses and Chincoteague ponies are very different.
    b. Assateague horses are tall, while Chincoteague ponies are short.
    c. Assateague horses and Chincoteague ponies are the same breed of horse.
    d. Assateague horses are nicer than Chincoteague ponies.

2. In paragraph five, the word "spectator" most likely means:
    a. A ghost
    b. Someone who watches
    c. A special event
    d. A pony

3. How are the north and south ends of Assateague Island the same?
    a. They are both in Virginia.
    b. They are both in Maryland.
    c. They both have pony sales.
    d. They both have a National Park.

4. This story is about:
    a. Two herds of horses on Assateague Island
    b. Learning how to sell ponies
    c. How Firefighters raise money for new equipment
    d. Learning how to make ponies swim

5. Although both herds live on Assateague Island, they are treated differently. What is the main difference?
    a. The Assateague horses are trained for riding.
    b. The Chincoteague ponies are given veterinary care.
    c. The Assateague horses are all solid colors.
    d. The Chincoteague ponies are all pinto patterns.

6. How might this story be different if it was told from the point of view of a Chincoteague pony?
    a. The reader might think the Chincoteague ponies were all over the island.
    b. The reader might think the Assateague horses were a different breed of horse.
    c. The reader might think that the ponies were full-sized horses.
    d. The reader might think the firefighters were just being mean to the ponies.

Katie's Journal

Every day after school, Katie writes in her journal. She writes about what happened during school that day and uses the journal to help express her feelings. This week has been very hard for Katie.

Monday

"Dear Diary, Today was just horrible! Sandy yelled at me after band class, and I don't even know why! I am not going to be her friend anymore!!!!"

Tuesday

"Dear Diary, Jenny says Sandy said mean things about me today in math class. I just want to hit Sandy. Why is she being so mean? Tomorrow I have science class with her, and band again. I just won't talk to her."

Wednesday

"Dear Diary, I wouldn't look at Sandy today, or talk to her. Science class was very quiet and tense, since she is my table partner. I did say, when I was talking to myself, that I sure wished I knew why SOME people were mad at me and being mean. She just sniffed and walked away."

Thursday

"Dear Diary, Jenny told me that Sandy said she was mad at me because I took her music folder out of her locker and lost one of the pages. I didn't touch her stupid music folder, and I sure didn't lose any pages. But...I can understand being upset about losing my music. We play the same instrument, so maybe I can help."

Friday

"Dear Diary, Today I took Sandy a copy of my music folder. My mom copied all the pages at her work yesterday, and I helped Sandy find the one she was missing and we replaced it. Sandy said she was sorry for talking about me to Jenny, and I apologized for not speaking to her in science. She is my best friend again."

Katie felt much better on Friday afternoon, knowing that she had saved her friendship with Sandy. Writing in her journal always helped her to think things out and make better decisions.

1. This story is about:
    a. Katie having a fight with her friend Sandy
    b. Katie and Jenny talking about other girls
    c. Jenny and Sandy becoming best friends
    d. How science class was very hard for Katie

2. What is the most likely meaning of "tense" in Wednesday's entry?
    a. Relaxed
    b. Strained
    c. Dramatic
    d. Quiet

3. How would the story be different without Friday's entry?
   a. The reader would know that Katie wasn't a nice person.
   b. The reader would think that Jenny was trying to break up Katie and Sandy's friendship.
   c. The reader wouldn't know that the fight had been resolved.
   d. The reader would think that Sandy and Katie were acting childish.

4. How would this story be different if it were told by an adult such the Katie's mom?
   a. The reader would not be able to know Katie's thoughts.
   b. The tone would be more amused than angry.
   c. It would have more excited language.
   d. It would be emotional.

5. At the beginning, Katie was very angry. How is she different by the end?
   a. Katie was angry, but she became calm.
   b. Katie was hurt, but she became angry.
   c. Katie was amused, but she became hurt.
   d. Katie was calm, but she became excited.

6. Which sentence is the best summary of Wednesday's entry?
   a. Even though they weren't speaking, Katie and Sandy worked together in science.
   b. Even though they weren't speaking, Katie and Sandy gave a presentation in science.
   c. Even though they weren't speaking, Katie and Sandy still found a way to be mean in science.
   d. Even though they weren't speaking, Katie and Sandy both failed science that day.

An Artist Thinking BIG

A sculpture can be made in many different sizes, from very tiny to very large. The largest sculptures are carved from whole mountains!

Three such mountain carvings have been done in the United States. Two are complete, and one is still being carved today. One artist, Gutzon Borglum, has a connection to all three sculptures.

Borglum first worked on Stone Mountain in Georgia. The Daughters of the Confederacy, a group of women whose ancestors were Rebel soldiers in the Civil War, asked Borglum to carve a 20 foot high bust of southern General Robert E. Lee in 1915. Borglum talked them into a much bigger bas-relief, or shallow relief, project, but before it could be finished he fought with the Daughters and left. It was finished by Augustus Lukeman and Walter Hancock and completed in 1972. Although Gutzon Borglum did not finish this mountain, he developed techniques such as a giant magic lantern projector to cast a drawing onto a mountain. Later he would use this technique on another famous carved mountain.

The most famous mountain carving is Mount Rushmore in South Dakota. The mountain has the faces of four famous and beloved American Presidents. George Washington, Thomas Jefferson, Theodore Roosevelt, and Abraham Lincoln look down from an enormous mountain in the Black Hills. Gutzon Borglum started the project in 1927, carving the four 60 foot high statues, until his death in 1941. His son, Lincoln Borglum, finished the mountain carving.

The third mountain carving is also in South Dakota, a short drive away from Mount Rushmore. The Crazy Horse Memorial, when finished, will be the largest sculpture in the world at 563 feet tall and 641 feet long. In 1939, Gutzon Borglum had an assistant artist named Korczack Ziolkowski working with him on the Mount Rushmore project. Chief Henry Standing Bear of the Lakota Sioux tribe asked Ziolkowski to carve the monument to show that Native Americans had heroes, too. Ziolkowski worked on the sculpture until his death in 1982. Now his wife Ruth and seven of their ten children are working to finish it.

Gutzon Borglum, and the artists that followed him, show us that no dreams are too big to become reality. One man, with the right vision, can change the world.

1. Which artist was connected to all three mountain carvings?
    a. Augustus Lukeman
    b. Lincoln Borglum
    c. Ruth Ziolkowski
    d. Gutzon Borglum

2. Which sentence is the best summary of paragraph 4?
    a. Mount Rushmore is the most famous of the three mountain carvings.
    b. Guzmon Borglum finished Mount Rushmore before he died.
    c. Mount Rushmore is the biggest sculpture in the world.
    d. Mount Rushmore has a hidden vault.

3. What do all three carvings have in common?
    a. All three carvings are finished today.
    b. All three carvings were finished by someone other than the original artist.
    c. All three carvings are bas-relief sculptures.
    d. All three carvings are in South Dakota.

4. In paragraph four, what is the most likely meaning of the word "enormous"?

   a. Small
   b. Huge
   c. Medium
   d. Unknown

5. This story is about:

   a. Three mountain carvings and the artist that connects them.
   b. How hard it is to finish a mountain carving.
   c. The artists who took over for Gutzon Borglum.
   d. How impossible it is for one person to change the world.

6. All three sculptures have common elements, but the Crazy Horse Memorial is different. How is it different?

   a. Crazy Horse is smaller than Mount Rushmore and Stone Mountain.
   b. Crazy Horse has no connection to Gutzon Borglum.
   c. Crazy Horse was finished by the original sculptor.
   d. Crazy Horse is the biggest and isn't finished yet.

The Disappearing Hair Ribbons

"I've lost more hair ribbons," Pilar said angrily. "That's the third ribbon this week that's disappeared." Pilar had beautiful long brown hair that she liked to wear braided with bright ribbons and bows on the end.

"Have you cleaned your room to look for them, Pilar?" asked Ms. Gonzales.

"I have, Mom, I looked under my bed and everything. Maybe if I ask Rosa to help, we can get to the bottom of this mystery," Pilar replied.

Rosa Morales lived next door to Pilar, and the two girls had been friends for years. Pilar and Rosa had started a detective agency last summer, and they had been hired by several neighbors to help solve mysteries at their house. The GoMo Detective Agency was becoming famous in their little neighborhood. Just last week, they had helped Marisol Lopez find her red rain boots.

When Pilar explained about her missing hair ribbons, Rosa quickly agreed to help. The GoMo Detective Agency was on the case!

"First, let's go to the scene of the crime," said Rosa, and they headed back to Pilar's bedroom.

Pilar had a four poster bed, a dresser, a night stand, and a desk in her room. She also had several pets: a hamster named Riley, a cat named Mrs. Piggy, and a ferret named Stinky. Riley lived in a closed hamster habitat with plastic trails to play in. Mrs. Piggy lived in the whole house, but she slept in Pilar's room every night. Stinky had a cage in Pilar's room that he slept in, but he was allowed to play in the room during the day.

"Okay, Pilar, I've got some questions for you," said Rosa as she got out her notebook to write down the answers. "First, who has been in your room since the first ribbon went missing? Second, have you searched all the furniture in the room? Third, where haven't you looked in the room? Fourth, what color are the ribbons?"

Pilar gave Rosa a list of the people who had been in her room. Mrs. Gonzales, Pilar's little brother Jaime, and Rosa were the only three people on the list. Pilar then told Rosa that she had searched all the furniture, inside and out, and even underneath! The third question made Pilar think hard for a few minutes, but there were only three places she hadn't searched yet: Riley's habitat, Stinky's cage, and the closet. The color of the missing ribbons was the easiest question. "One is blue, one is pink, and one is yellow," Pilar told Rosa.

The girls decided to search those places before they questioned any of their suspects. Riley's habitat was small and easy to search. While Rosa held Riley, Pilar lifted up his bowls and his house and ran her fingers through the pine chips on the bottom, but she didn't find anything. Next, Pilar held Stinky while Rosa did the same in his cage. She searched under his house, his bed, and in his food dish. The only place left was the closet. Pilar let Stinky run loose around the room while the girls searched.

Pilar took the shelves to search and Rosa took the floor. Stinky seemed to want to help too. He headed straight into the closet when it was opened.

After a few moments, Rosa started laughing and pointed to Pilar's boots. Stinky's back legs and the ends of a blue ribbon were poking out of it.

GoMo Detective Agency solved another mystery!

1. What is the most likely definition of the word "suspects"?
    a. Someone who is thought to be silly
    b. Someone who is thought to be guilty
    c. Someone who is thought to be angry
    d. Someone who is thought to be innocent

2. Why is it easier for Rosa to think of the right questions to ask?
    a. Pilar is upset.
    b. Pilar is not as smart as Rosa.
    c. Rosa is older.
    d. Rosa is angry.

*Read the sentences below. Choose **B** if the event happened before Rosa agreed to help, and **A** if it happened after.*

3. Pilar's ribbons went missing.

4. Rosa searched Riley's habitat.

5. Stinky climbed in Pilar's boot.

6. What is the best summary of paragraph 4?
    a. Pilar and Rosa had been friends for a year.
    b. Pilar and Rosa were nosy.
    c. Pilar and Rosa were neighborhood detectives.
    d. Pilar and Rosa had been detectives since they were little.

Animals of Yellowstone

Jason and his family are visiting Yellowstone National Park in Wyoming. Jason and his sister, Jennifer, are hoping to see some of the more special mammals that live in the park. Jason and Jennifer love photography and want to take pictures of the animals. The week before their trip, Jason had prepared a chart so they could figure out the best places to look for each animal and how likely they were to see them.

Animal	Habitat	Likely Location in the Park	Population
Grizzly Bear	forests, meadows	Lamar Valley, Mt. Washburn, Hayden Valley, Mammoth Hot Springs	500 - 650
Black Bear	forests, meadows	Lamar Valley, Mt. Washburn, Hayden Valley, Mammoth Hot Springs	280 - 610
Gray Wolf	forests, meadows	Lamar Valley, Mt. Washburn, Hayden Valley, Mammoth Hot Springs	less than 100
Elk	forests, meadows	Lamar Valley, Mt. Washburn, Hayden Valley, Mammoth Hot Springs, Old Faithful	15,000 - 25,000
Moose	river banks, forests	South Entrance, West Thumb	less than 500
Bison	meadows, grasslands	Lamar Valley, Mt. Washburn, Hayden Valley, Mammoth Hot Springs, Old Faithful	less than 3,500
Big Horn Sheep	cliffs, mountain slopes	Mt. Washburn, Mammoth Hot Springs	250 - 275

1. Why did Jason research the Yellowstone Animals?
    a. He wanted to know which animals lived in the park.
    b. He wanted to impress his sister.
    c. He wanted to find out how many animals there were.
    d. He wanted to know where to look for the animals.

2. Where are Jason and Jennifer most likely to see moose?
    a. South Entrance and West Thumb
    b. Lamar Valley and Mt. Washburn
    c. Mammoth Hot Springs and Hayden Valley
    d. South Entrance and Old Faithful

3. Which animal has the largest population?
    a. Moose
    b. Elk
    c. Gray Wolf
    d. Grizzly Bear

4. Information in this passage suggests
    a. Big Horn sheep live in more areas than any other animal.
    b. There are more grey wolves than moose.
    c. More animals live in forests and meadows.
    d. There are more predators than prey in the park.

5. From the context of this passage, what does the word "habitat" mean?
    a. A regular or usual action
    b. An unfamiliar area
    c. A place where animals store food for the winter
    d. An animal's home area

6. What evidence does the author give suggesting they will NOT see any grey wolves?
    a. The wolves live in forests and meadows.
    b. The wolves have the smallest population.
    c. The wolves live in meadows and grasslands.
    d. The wolves can be seen in Lamar Valley.

A Day in the City

Robby and his dad planned to spend Saturday in Washington, D.C. They had several stops planned, including Pentagon City, Arlington National Cemetery, and the Smithsonian. Because it costs so much to park in the city, Robby and his father take the subway the first Saturday of every month when they have a "boy's day" together.

"We have to look at a subway system map and make a chart so we can figure out which one is the best to use," said Robby's dad. "There are five different subway lines in the city: red, blue, orange, green, and yellow."

	Red Line	Blue Line	Orange Line	Green Line	Yellow Line
Pentagon City		x			x
The White House		x	X		
Smithsonian		x	X		
National Zoo	x				
National Archives				x	x
Arlington Cemetery		x			
National Air and Space Museum		x	X	x	x
International Spy Museum	x			x	x
Washington National Cathedral	x				

1. How will Robby and his dad get to all the places on their list?
    a. Walk
    b. Bus
    c. Car
    d. Subway

2. Robby and his dad can use the subway chart to help answer which of the following questions?
    a. What time does the subway arrive at the White House?
    b. How much does it cost to take the subway?
    c. Which subway lines would you take to get to the National Archives?
    d. How long will it take to get to Pentagon City?

3. Which of these best describes Robby and his father?
    a. They don't like to drive in the city.
    b. They enjoy doing things together.
    c. They think the subway schedule is too complicated.
    d. They think the subway is dirty and crowded.

4. Which of the following places could Robby and his dad visit while staying on **the same** subway line?

a. The National Zoo and the Pentagon City
b. The National Archives and the Washington National Cathedral
c. The White House and the National Air and Space Museum
d. Washington National Cathedral and Arlington Cemetery

5. Read the following dictionary entry for the word "chart."

Chart (*chahrt*) n. 1. a sheet arranging information into columns or tabs; 2. a map, especially a marine map; 3. a graphic representation; 4. an outline map showing special conditions or facts, such as a weather chart.

Which definition represents the meaning of "chart" as used in the passage?

a. Definition 1
b. Definition 2
c. Definition 3
d. Definition 4

6. What evidence does the author use to suggest that the Washington National Cathedral is a difficult location to reach?

a. It is only on one subway line.
b. The blue line has many more attractions.
c. Robby and his dad are not planning to go there.
d. It is near the International Spy Museum.

Family Names

Surnames are names that families share. They are passed down from generation to generation today, but this was not always the case.

Last names were first used in Europe during the middle Ages. People only had first names, so if three men named John lived in your village, it could get very confusing! However, if one John was a baker, one was an archer, and one was a barrel maker, you could tell them apart by calling them by their profession. John the baker became John Baker, John the archer became John Archer, and John the barrel maker became John Cooper.

Does your family name come from a job your ancestors had long ago?

Last Name	Occupation	Origin
Bender	Bow Maker	This name comes from the Old English word "bendbow," for someone who makes bows for archery.
Cartwright	Cart Maker/Repairer	People named Cartwright were early transportation engineers.
Fletcher	Arrow Maker/Seller	Fletcher comes from the French word "fleche," which means arrow.
Mason	Stone Worker	Masons built brick and stone buildings such as castles.
Parker	Gamekeeper	Parkers took care of the woodlands and wildlife, much like a park ranger today.
Saddler	Saddle Maker	This person made saddles for horses.
Steward	Manager	The word "steward" comes from Middle English and was the title of the person who managed someone else's estate or home.

1. What is the main idea of this chart?
    a. To explain family names based on a person's father
    b. To explain European family names from the Dark Ages
    c. To explain family names based on occupations
    d. To explain family names based on different languages

2. From the passage, the word "transportation" most likely means
   a. To move people or things
   b. To build ships
   c. To build wheels
   d. To ship items to another place

3. What evidence does the chart give to support the idea that last names come from occupations?
   a. Lists of famous people with those last names
   b. Lists the first person ever to use the name and their occupation
   c. Definitions of colors and their meanings
   d. Definitions and origins of occupational words

4. According to this passage, if your last name is Cook, your ancestor most likely
   a. Was a pig keeper.
   b. Was a chef.
   c. Was a candle maker.
   d. Was a beer maker.

5. Two of the last names are from related occupations. Which two?
   a. Fletcher and Bender
   b. Cartwright and Mason
   c. Parker and Steward
   d. Steward and Cartwright

6. From the passage, "surname" most likely means
   a. Manager
   b. Middle Ages
   c. Last Name
   d. Occupation

Meteor Watching

Every year in August, the Perseid Meteor shower is visible to the naked eye and is a favorite for professional and amateur astronomers, alike.

Many people like the Perseid Meteor shower because it happens in the summer when people are on vacation, the nighttime temperatures are moderate, and the weather generally is good. People have been enjoying this summer sky show for over 2,000 years.

Meteors are little bits of rock and ice left over from a comet passing by. The Perseid meteors are from the comet Swift-Tuttle, which passes by Earth every 135 years. The comet leaves a debris trail through which the Earth passes every year on its way around the Sun.

As the Earth moves through the debris trail, the meteors hit the atmosphere and burn, leaving streaks of light across the sky. The best time to see this light show is in the very early morning when the moon is setting. You need to be away from city lights, with a dark, open sky to see the shooting stars at their best.

1. Which of the following choices gives the main idea of the passage?
   a. The meteor shower is boring.
   b. Watching meteor showers in the country is easy.
   c. The Perseid meteor shower is a favorite.
   d. Watching meteor showers in the city is hard.

2. What evidence does the author give to suggest that the Perseid shower only happens once a year?
   a. It only happens in August.
   b. The comet only passes by every 135 years.
   c. People have been watching the shower for 2000 years.
   d. The weather is good for the shower.

3. From the passage, what does the word "debris" most likely mean?
   a. A collection of things
   b. A comet's tail
   c. Scattered fragments of rock
   d. The orbit around the Sun.

4. Both the Earth and the Swift-Tuttle comet orbit the sun. What is the major difference between their orbits?

a. The Earth is a planet with an atmosphere.
b. The comet has two names.
c. The comet has a debris trail.
d. The Earth takes one year to orbit the sun, and the comet takes 135 years to orbit the sun.

5. What is the best summary of paragraph 2?

a. People have enjoyed watching the shower for 2000 years.
b. People enjoy watching the shower because it happens in the summer.
c. People enjoy moderate temperatures.
d. People enjoy being on vacation.

6. From the passage, what does the word "moderate" most likely mean?

a. Extreme
b. Average
c. Mild
d. Nonexistent

Reading: Foundational Skills

Parts of Words

Many words in English are made up of small parts put together. These parts include a root word and possibly one or more affixes. Prefixes and suffixes change the meaning of the root word. The meaning could change a little or a lot, depending on the affix added.

Root Words

The root is the main part of the word. It has the most meaning in the word. For example, the word midnight has two parts: mid- and night. The root of midnight is night.

In each of the following questions, underline the root of the word.

1. bicycle

2. comfortable

3. biologist

4. refill

5. prearrange

Affixes

Affixes are parts of words that can be added to the beginning or end of a root word to change the meaning. Prefixes are added to the beginning of a word. Suffixes are added to the end. For example, un- is a prefix that means "not." So, "unprepared" means not prepared. If you add a suffix such as -ness to the end of a word, then prepared becomes preparedness, which means feeling prepared. The affixes really change the meanings.

Prefixes

*In the questions below, underline the **prefix** and then choose the definition that most closely fits the WHOLE word.*

1. irresponsible
    a. very responsible
    b. great responsibility
    c. lacking responsibility
    d. kind of responsible

2. antifreeze
    a. a liquid used to freeze other liquids
    b. a liquid used to keep other liquids from freezing
    c. a liquid used to freeze ice cubes.
    d. a liquid used to keep food from freezing.

3. impossible
    a. not able to occur
    b. unwanted outcome
    c. able to occur
    d. desired outcome

4. mistake
    a. a happy thing.
    b. a correct thing.
    c. an excitement
    d. an error

5. prehistoric
    a. before historians
    b. before written records
    c. after written records
    d. after history books

Suffixes

Suffixes are affixes that go at the end of the word. For example, if you add -hood to neighbor, you get neighborhood. So instead of "a person who lives next door," you get "a community." Big difference!

*For the questions below, underline the **suffix** and then choose the definition that most closely fits the WHOLE word.*

1. properly
   a. in the right manner
   b. in a serious manner
   c. in the wrong manner
   d. in a silly manner

2. joyful
   a. feeling or causing sorrow
   b. feeling or causing happiness
   c. feeling or causing pain
   d. feeling or causing noise

3. scientist
   a. a person who does magic tricks
   b. a person who writes books
   c. a person who studies science
   d. a person who sings songs

4. musician
   a. a person who plays soccer
   b. a person who cannot sing
   c. a person who writes about sports
   d. a person who plays music

5. excitement
    a. a feeling of eagerness
    b. a feeling of sadness
    c. a feeling of longing
    d. a feeling of loneliness

Writing

Nebraska Pioneer Children

Life as a pioneer in Nebraska was not easy. Most families farmed and lived in sod houses or log cabins. They didn't have electricity or running water. These pioneers faced many challenges, and these challenges were hard especially for the children. Prairie farmers often could not afford to hire adult helpers, so they relied on their children to help.

Children arose early, while it was still dark, to begin their chores. Some chores even had to be done before breakfast. Different seasons called for different chores. Boys learned to plant and harvest crops. They hunted and fished to provide food for the family. Sometimes they gathered cow or buffalo chips to use as fuel for the fire. Girls helped with gathering eggs, cooking, cleaning the house, mending clothes and socks, and taking care of the younger children.

School was a challenge, as well. Many children were taught at home because they were needed to help at home. Without the children, the farm would not have survived. Children who did go to school went every day except Sunday, from October to May. That way, they could be home during the planting and harvesting seasons.

Eighth grade was the highest level, and all grades were taught together in one room. School supplies were scarce and expensive, so instead of paper and pencils, most students learned to write and did their lessons on slates.

For each of the following questions, be sure to use examples or facts from the story to support your answer. Edit your work for correct grammar and punctuation. Remember to include an introduction and conclusion.

1. Choose **one** aspect of life for pioneer children and write about what surprised you the most.

2. Explain why pioneer children had to work so hard.

3. Imagine you could go back to pioneer days in Nebraska. What three objects would you take with you and why?

4. Compare and contrast the chores of boys and girls in a pioneer household. Why were they different?

The Olympics, Past and Present

The ancient Greeks started the Olympic Games on the plains of Olympia in Peloponnesus, Greece. The games were dedicated to the god, Zeus.

The first games were held almost 3000 years ago in 776 BC. Back then, the Olympics consisted of only one game, a short sprint called a "stade." Only men ran the race, and they ran in the nude. In fact, women could not even watch the games, much less compete in them, because the games were held to honor Zeus and therefore only for men. An olive branch wreath was placed on the winner's head, because the olive tree was sacred in Athens, Greece. .

The games were held every four years, and the period in between the games was called the Olympiad. For 1,170 years, the Greeks held the Olympics every four years. As time went on, more events were added, including racing, wrestling, boxing, equestrian events (such as chariot races), and the pentathlon, which consisted of five track and field events (long jump, javelin throw, discus throw, foot races, and wrestling).

The Olympic Flame began in the original games, as well. To symbolize the death and rebirth of ancient Greek heroes as well as the time when Prometheus stole fire from the gods, a flame was lit at the beginning of each Olympics and kept burning until the games were completed.

Unfortunately, the Olympics were banned by Emperor Theodosius II in 394 AD.

In 1896, a Frenchman named Pierre de Coubertin organized a new Olympic games in Athens, Greece. These games featured 12 athletic events, including a marathon. Fourteen nations sent athletes, and all the athletes were male. Women began competing in the 1900 Olympics in Paris. The Olympics continued every four years, but they did not return to Greece for another 108 years. In 1924, the first Winter Olympics were held in France.

Today, the Olympics still happen every four years, but they are split into the Summer and Winter Games. The top athletes, men and women alike, compete for medals—gold for first place, silver for second place, and bronze for third place. Furthermore, the Olympics feature both solo events and team events. An average of 200 nations and over 10,000 athletes compete at every Olympics now.

The Summer Olympics include events such as archery, baseball, boxing, cycling, diving, equestrian, soccer, gymnastics, and many more. The Winter Olympics have different events such as ice hockey, figure skating, snowboarding, bobsleigh, skiing, and a biathlon (skiing and shooting).

The Olympic flame still burns. It is lit at the site of the ancient Olympic Games in Greece several months before the opening ceremonies. A parabolic mirror is used to focus the Sun's rays and light the torch. Then, runners carry the torch around Greece and transfer the flame to the host country. Until 2008, the torch was carried through many countries before reaching the host, but today it is given directly to the country where the Olympic Games are being held. The final runner lights the Olympic Flame with the torch. Just like in ancient times, the flame stays lit until the games are complete.

For each of the following questions, be sure to use examples or facts from the story to support your answer. Edit your work for correct grammar and punctuation. Remember to include an introduction and conclusion.

1. Compare and contrast the ancient Olympics with the modern Olympics.

____

____

____

____

____

____

2. Imagine that an athlete from the ancient Olympics could compete today. What events would he want to compete in and why?

____

____

____

____

____

____

3. Why you think there are now Summer and Winter Olympic Games? Use examples from the text to support your idea.

____

____

____

____

____

4. Pretend that you have to give a presentation to your classmates about the Olympics. Write your speech, using examples and quotes from the passage above.

Writing Answer Key

Nebraska Pioneer Children

1. Answers will vary.

2. Answers will vary, but should include: no electricity, food for survival, farmers were poor, so they could not afford to hire adult helpers, etc.

3. Answers will vary.

4. Boys: planting and harvesting, hunting and fishing, gathering fuel for the fire. Girls: cooking and cleaning, mending clothing, taking care of children. Answers might include physical strength, societal pressures, preparation for having a farm/husband/wife of their own one day.

The Olympics, Past and Present

1. Answers should include such elements as: Ancient were men only, they were summer only, they were conducted nude, games only included track and field type games, and they were a religious celebration. Modern are men and women, athletes wear clothing, there are MANY more events and games, they are both summer and winter.

2. Answer will vary.

3. Answers will vary.

4. Answers will vary.

Language

Prepositions

Prepositions show the relationship of a noun or pronoun to another word or phrase. They show direction, position, or other relationships. An easy way to remember is to think about a cat. A preposition is almost anywhere a cat can go.

For the following sentences, underline the preposition in each one.

1. Nick ran between Nate and Evan on the playground
2. Nate leaped over Evan playing leapfrog.
3. Evan climbed across the monkey bars.
4. Nate ran toward the slides.
5. Evan and Nick rode around on the merry go round.

Conjunctions

Conjunctions are connecting words that connect different parts of a sentence.

There are three kinds of conjunctions. **Coordinating conjunctions** help to connect two equal parts of a sentence; **subordinating conjunctions** connect a dependent clause to a main clause; and **correlative conjunctions** are *pairs of words* that link balanced words or phrases.

Examples:
Coordinating: Nick *and* Evan went to the playground.
Subordinating: Nate can't go swimming *until* they come back.
Correlative: *Both* Evan *and* Nick wanted to ride dirt bikes.

For the following sentences, underline the conjunction and then write whether the conjunction is coordinating, subordinating, or correlative.

1. Nick and Nate rode their dirt bikes through the woods.

2. Evan waited to ride because there were only two bikes.

3. Neither Nate nor Evan can drive a car yet.

4. Nate wanted to ride over the ramp, although it was too high.

5. Nick wants to eat not only pizza, but also hamburgers.

6. Evan wants to go to the movies, but Nick wants to go swimming.

7. Nate would like to have hamburgers and pizza for lunch.

8. Either Evan or Nick can ride the larger dirt bike.

9. The boys will go swimming unless it's too cold.

10. Both Nate and Evan are twins.

Verb Tenses

Verbs are words that show action. For example, in the sentence "Nate ate his hamburger," “ate” is the verb because it shows what Nate did.

The tense of a verb tells you when the action takes place.

- The verb is in the present tense if the action is happening now.
- The verb is in the past tense if the action already has happened.
- The verb is in the future tense if the action is going to happen.

Examples:
Present: Nate licks his ice cream cone.
Past: Evan ate his hamburger.
Future: Nick will drink his soda after lunch.

For the sentences below, decide if the action is happening in the present, happened in the past, or will happen in the future. Underline the verb and choose the correct tense.

1. Nate and Evan will go to Vietnam this spring.
   a. Present
   b. Past
   c. Future

2. Their grandmother cooks pho noodles for the boys.
   a. Present
   b. Past
   c. Future

3. Last year, it rained every day they were in Vietnam.
   a. Present
   b. Past
   c. Future

4. The boys will visit Tran Quoc Pagoda this year.
   a. Present
   b. Past
   c. Future

5. Their grandmother lives outside of Hanoi, the capital city of Vietnam.
   a. Present
   b. Past
   c. Future

For the following sentences, write the verb in its correct tense in the blank.

6. The boys ____________ (ride) the train last year.

7. Nick ____________ (enjoy) watching the scenery from the train windows.

8. Evan ____________ (read) a book if they take the train again.

9. Nate ____________ (want) to fly last year.

10. All three boys ____________ (play) checkers if they ride the train.

Capitalization

Some words need to be capitalized. For this reason, there are rules to help you remember which words need capitalization. Capitalizing can be confusing, so a good rule of thumb is that words are capitalized if they are unique persons, places or things (nouns!), if they start a sentence, or if they are the important word in a title.

Some Capitalization Rules:

- The first word of every sentence
- Names of persons, months, days, holidays, countries, states, and cities
- Initials used in names and well-known organizations
- The word "I"
- Titles of books, songs, or people

For the following sentences, circle yes if the underlined word needs to be capitalized and no if it doesn't need to be capitalized.

1. <u>jenny</u> and Kim want to have a sleepover. Yes / No

2. They have planned the party for <u>friday</u> night. Yes / No

3. "Let me know if your <u>mom</u> says we can have it at your house," said Kim. Yes / No

4. "She will, <u>i</u> am sure of it," replied Jenny.

Yes
No

5. The next school holiday is <u>thanksgiving</u>.

Yes
No

6. Jenny's mom works for the county <u>judge</u>.

Yes
No

7. Her boss, <u>judge</u> Johnson, is very nice.

Yes
No

8. Kim's favorite band is Ben <u>folds</u> Five.

Yes
No

Punctuation

Periods, Questions Marks and Exclamation Points - Ending Punctuation

There are three main types of sentences: declarative, interrogative, and exclamatory. The ending punctuation you choose to put on a sentence changes the type of sentence it becomes.

- **Declarative sentences** make a statement. A **period (.)** is the correct ending punctuation for a declarative sentence.
- **Interrogative sentences** ask a question. A question mark (?) is the correct ending punctuation for an interrogative sentence.
- **Exclamatory sentences** express excitement or deep emotion. An **exclamation point (!)** is the correct ending punctuation for an exclamatory sentence.

Read the sentences below and decide if the sentence is making a statement, asking a question, or expressing emotion.

1. What time does the game start ____________________

2. I returned my books to the library ____________________

3. Mom is making your favorite dinner tonight ____________________

4. Jason, your house is on fire ____________________

5. Is Nate your best friend ____________________

6. I love you ____________________

7. Nick, can we play at your house ____________________

8. Mr. Kessler's store sells school supplies ____________________

9. Where is your bicycle ____________________

10. That boy stole my bicycle ____________________

Commas

Commas are punctuation, too. A comma (,) tells the reader to pause for a moment, but not to stop completely. There are lots of rules for commas, depending on the situation.

A Few Rules for Commas

- Commas separate a series of three or more words or phrases. (*She likes dolls, ponies, and kittens.*)
- Commas are used in dates between the day and year (*December 7, 1941*) and after the year if there is more to the sentence. (*On December 7, 1941, the Japanese attacked Pearl Harbor.*)

- Commas separate the name of a city and the name of its state or country (*Dallas, Texas*) or if there is more of the sentence after the state. (*We were in Dallas, Texas, last month.*)
- Commas separate two independent clauses before the coordinating conjunction. (*Sarah was hungry, yet nothing sounded good to eat.)*
- Commas separate a dependent clause from an independent clause at the beginning of a sentence. (*Due to a flash flood, we were not able to play street hockey.*)
- Commas separate additional information that could be removed from the sentence without changing its meaning. (*Joey, the boy in the third row, finished his homework.*)
- Commas show pauses in the sentence. (*Outside, the boxes were stacked in rows.*)
- Commas separate Yes and No and tag questions. (*Yes, I would like another piece of pie. No, thank you, I have had enough. It's true, isn't it?*)
- Commas separate direct quotes from the information that introduces or explains the quote. (*"Please don't forget to put your papers on my desk," said the teacher.*)
- Commas separate introductory phrases of four or more words. (*At the end of the month, we will meet our quota.*)

Write the following sentences correctly by adding commas where they belong.

1. In Houston Texas there is a huge rodeo in February.

2. Johnny said "Let's go play on the swings."

3. It's going to rain today isn't it?

4. Nate had three apples two oranges and a banana in his lunch box.

5. Eureka a show on the SyFy channel is about a town of geniuses.

6. The Revolutionary War officially ended on May 12 1784.

7. Yes thank you I would love some cake.

8. Along with his friends Evan thought he could help others.

9. Because of the lightning we could not play outside.

10. We can vacation at the beach or we can go to the city.

Write two sentences of your own about music. Use a series in one sentence and a date in the other.

11. ____

____

____

____

____

12. ____

____

____

____

____

Titles

Titles can be confusing. Sometimes they are underlined, sometimes in italics, and sometimes in quotation marks.

Rules for Titles:

- Short works (such as the title of an article or a short poem) and parts of longer works (such as the title of a chapter) are usually in quotation marks. (*Title of a short story, "Young Goodman Brown")*
- Long works (such as books, movies, television series, or albums) and collections of works (magazines, newspapers, anthologies) are placed in italics. You also can underline INSTEAD of using italics, but not both together. (Title of a Television series*:* iCarly *or* Title of a movie*: Star Wars Episode I)*

Punctuate the titles in the sentences below correctly by using quotations marks or by underlining.

1. To Kill a Mockingbird is my favorite novel.

2. The headline read, Man Kills Seven in Subway.

3. My class went to see An Ideal Husband, a play by Oscar Wilde.

4. The Avengers was the best movie this summer!

5. What Sarah Said, by Death Cab for Cutie, is the best song ever.

Changing Sentences

To keep your reader interested, you need to have a variety of sentences. Some of them should be long, some short, some simple, and some complex.

Rules for changing sentences:

- You can combine two short sentences by moving key words and phrases from one sentence to another. (*The aquarium is full of small fish. It is in my bedroom. Combined: The aquarium in my bedroom is full of small fish.*)

- You can combine sentence with related ideas to make compound or complex sentences. To do this, you use conjunctions such as *and*, *or*, and *because*. (I am happy. I see a puppy. Combined: I am happy because I see a puppy.)

For the sentence pairs below, combine them to make more interesting sentences.

1. Nate and Evan go to the Houston Zoo. They go on Sundays.

____

____

2. Dragonflies live by the river. I am hoping to see some today.

____

____

3. Evan likes the monkeys. The monkeys live in the primate habitat.

____

____

4. Baboons are from African and Asia. They mostly live in zoos now.

____

____

5. Nick watches the baby giraffe. It tries to eat leaves from a tall tree.

____

____

Multiple Meaning Words

Some words have more than one meaning. There are two types of multiple meaning words: those that sound alike, or those that sound different.

- Words that sound alike
    - Homophones sound alike but are spelled differently. (*I* ***so*** *want to* ***sew*** *that button for you.*)
- Words that sound different
    - Heteronyms are spelled the same but sound different. (*It's hard to drive a* ***windy*** *road on a* ***windy*** *day.)*

Homophones:

For the questions below, circle the correct homophone to match the meaning.

1. 9 minus 7	too	two
2. correct	write	right
3. not here but	there	they're
4. less than two	one	won
5. tossed	through	threw
6. make a mistake	air	err
7. walkway	isle	aisle
8. chewed and swallowed	ate	eight
9. deep or low	bass	base
10. uncovered	bare	bear

Heteronyms

Read the sentences below and circle the correct heteronym to fit the meaning in parenthesis.

1. The Polish furniture needs polish. (a substance to give a shiny surface)

2. I object to that object. (disapprove)

3. She was too close to the window to close it. (to shut)

4. The bass drum had a bass painted on it. (a fish)

5. Mr. Jones is ready to present the present to the President. (to give formally)

6. Don't desert us just because we are in the desert. (to leave)

7. The dove dove for the food. (a bird)

8. Give me a minute and I'll show you minute particles in my microscope. (tiny)

9. The Grateful Dead are here to record a new record. (to preserve in sound)

10. I refuse to take out the refuse. (to say no)

Greek and Latin roots and affixes

Earlier, you worked with some common root words and affixes (prefixes and suffixes). Knowing what the root word means, or understanding the affix, can help you to figure out the meaning of a new word.

For the sentences below, the Greek / Latin root or affix and its meaning have been provided. The sentences use a variation of this root word. Use the meaning of the Greek / Latin word to help you place the correct modern word in the right sentence.

1. Photo = light

photograph   telephoto   photosynthesis   photogenic

a. She certainly is ______________________________.

b. My new camera takes a great ______________________________.

c. This big lens helps take ______________________________ shots.

d. Plants use ______________________________ to make food.

2. Aero = air

aerobics   aerodynamics   aeronautics   aerate

a. The study of wind flow over an object is called __________________.

b. My mom takes a(n) __________________. exercise class.

c. Poke holes in the soil to __________________. the roots of the plant.

d. Scientist use __________________. to improve plane and space flight.

3. Dem = people

democracy demography endemic epidemic

a. When a lot of people catch the same disease, they call it a(n) ______________________.

b. America's form of government is a(n) ______________________.

c. The study of vital statistics such as birth rates is called __________________.

d. A(n) ______________________ disease is found in a particular place or people.

Context Clues

Learning how to guess words you don't know is an important skill, and one of the best ways to do that is with context clues. Use the rest of the sentence, or even the whole paragraph to figure out what an unfamiliar word might mean.

For the questions below, read the sentence and use context clues to choose the most likely meaning for the underlined word.

1. Robert's pet snake slithered across the floor.
   a. moved
   b. stopped
   c. hunted
   d. chased

2. We should abolish the "no hats" rule in class.
   a. start
   b. get rid of
   c. comply with
   d. agree with

3. I feel <u>deprived</u> when I can't play my guitar.
    a. damaged
    b. challenged
    c. happy
    d. denied

4. Wind Cave is <u>immense</u>! I can't see the top!
    a. huge
    b. small
    c. damp
    d. dark

5. The spy was very <u>nonchalant</u> as he walked slowly through the White House.
    a. happy
    b. sad
    c. calm
    d. excited

Reference Materials

Sometimes, to find the meaning of a word or learn how to pronounce it, you have to use reference materials. Reference materials can include dictionaries, encyclopedias, glossaries, or thesauruses.

For the questions below, a dictionary entry has been provided for you. Read it carefully and then answer the questions.

(1) **Miniature** . (2) [ˈmin(ē)əCHər]   (3)**adj.** of a much smaller size than normal

  noun. a thing that is much smaller than normal

  verb. represent on a smaller scale

(4)synonyms: diminutive, tiny, small

1. Which part of the entry tells you how to pronounce the word?
   a. 1
   b. 2
   c. 3
   d. 4

2. Which part of the entry tells you the definition(s) of the word?
   a. 1
   b. 2
   c. 3
   d. 4

3. Which part of the entry gives you words that have similar meanings?
   a. 1
   b. 2
   c. 3
   d. 4

4. Which part of the entry shows you how to spell the word correctly?
   a. 1
   b. 2
   c. 3
   d. 4

For the following questions, indicate which type of reference you would use to find the requested information.

a. Dictionary b. Glossary c. Thesaurus d. Encyclopedia

5. Where could you find out more information about Los Dios de Muertos?

6. Where could you find out the definition of the word *narrator*?

7. Where could you find words with similar meanings to the word *protagonist*?

8. Where would you look to find out the meaning of an underlined word in your science book?

Figurative Language

Authors use figurative language such as similes, metaphors, alliteration, idioms, and onomatopoeia to help the reader paint a picture in their minds.

Simile - compares two ideas, feelings, or things using "like" or "as"
Ex: Float like a butterfly
Metaphor - compares two ideas, feelings, or things without "like" or "as"
Ex: The night sky is black velvet.
Alliteration - repetition of beginning sounds
Ex: Al ate apples all around Albany.
Onomatopoeia - the words that represent a sound
Ex: Boom!
Idiom - a natural form of expression
Ex: Out of the blue

Read the following sentences and choose the correct form of figurative language.

1. I've been working like a dog.
   a. simile
   b. metaphor
   c. alliteration
   d. onomatopoeia
   e. idiom

2. The dog barked and howled all night.
   a. simile
   b. metaphor
   c. alliteration
   d. onomatopoeia
   e. idiom

3. Don't buy that. Red scarves are a dime a dozen.
   a. simile
   b. metaphor
   c. alliteration
   d. onomatopoeia
   e. idiom

4. Geoffrey has the heart of a lion.
   a. simile
   b. metaphor
   c. alliteration
   d. onomatopoeia
   e. idiom

5. Suzie sells seashells by the sea shore.
   a. simile
   b. metaphor
   c. alliteration
   d. onomatopoeia
   e. idiom

Synonyms and Antonyms

Another way authors keep their readers' interest is by using synonyms and antonyms. This keeps them from using the same words over and over.

Synonyms are words with nearly the same meaning as another word. (reply/answer)
Antonyms are words with opposite meanings. (wrong/right)

*For each of the sentences below, write a **synonym** for the underlined word.*

1. The <u>large</u> dog jumped on the fence. ________________

2. Math is very difficult. ________________

3. Jack and Jill went up the hill with a pail. ________________

4. Nate's dad was very angry with the boys. ________________

5. "Don't speak to me," said Julia. ________________

For each of the sentences below, write an ***antonym*** *for the underlined word.*

6. I love living in the country. ________________

7. The cookie jar is always empty. ________________

8. That dog is ugly! ________________

9. You have to freeze popsicles before you eat them.________________

10. Throw me the ball! ________________

Practice Test #1

Practice Questions

Question 1-5 pertain to the following excerpt from Alice's Adventures in Wonderland by Lewis Carroll:

Chapter 1: Down the Rabbit Hole

Alice was beginning to get very tired of sitting by her sister on the bank, and of having nothing to do: once or twice she had peeped into the book her sister was reading, but it had no pictures or conversations in it, 'and what is the use of a book,' thought Alice 'without pictures or conversation?'

So she was considering in her own mind (as well as she could, for the hot day made her feel very sleepy and stupid), whether the pleasure of making a daisy-chain would be worth the trouble of getting up and picking the daisies, when suddenly a White Rabbit with pink eyes ran close by her.

There was nothing so very remarkable in that; nor did Alice think it so very much out of the way to hear the Rabbit say to itself, 'Oh dear! Oh dear! I shall be late!' (when she thought it over afterwards, it occurred to her that she ought to have wondered at this, but at the time it all seemed quite natural); but when the Rabbit actually took a watch out of its waistcoat-pocket, and looked at it, and then hurried on, Alice started to her feet, for it flashed across her mind that she had never before seen a rabbit with either a waistcoat-pocket, or a watch to take out of it, and burning with curiosity, she ran across the field after it, and fortunately was just in time to see it pop down a large rabbit-hole under the hedge.

In another moment down went Alice after it, never once considering how in the world she was to get out again.

The rabbit-hole went straight on like a tunnel for some way, and then dipped suddenly down, so suddenly that Alice had not a moment to think about stopping herself before she found herself falling down a very deep well.

Either the well was very deep, or she fell very slowly, for she had plenty of time as she went down to look about her and to wonder what was going to happen next. First, she tried to look down and make out what she was coming to, but it was too dark to see anything; then she looked at the sides of the well, and noticed that they were filled with cupboards and book-shelves; here and there she saw maps and pictures hung upon pegs. She took down a jar from one of the shelves as she passed; it was labeled 'ORANGE MARMALADE', but to her great disappointment it was empty: she did not like to drop the jar for fear of killing somebody, so managed to put it into one of the cupboards as she fell past it.

'Well!' thought Alice to herself, 'after such a fall as this, I shall think nothing of tumbling down stairs! How brave they'll all think me at home! Why, I wouldn't say anything about it, even if I fell off the top of the house!' (Which was very likely true.)

1. Which line from the passage shows that Alice didn't think the talking rabbit was very strange?

Ⓐ 'and what is the use of a book,' thought Alice 'without pictures or conversation?'

Ⓑ as well as she could, for the hot day made her feel very sleepy and stupid

Ⓒ nor did Alice think it so very much out of the way to hear the Rabbit say to itself, 'Oh dear! Oh dear! I shall be late!'

Ⓓ In another moment down went Alice after it, never once considering how in the world she was to get out again.

2. Which answer best shows what happens in the passage?

Ⓐ Alice sits next to her sister on a riverbank when she starts to feel sleepy.

Ⓑ Alice jumps down a well and sees some shelves as she falls.

Ⓒ Alice meets a talking rabbit and becomes very good friends with it.

Ⓓ Alice sees a talking rabbit and follows it into a very, very deep hole.

3. How is Alice's world in the first two paragraphs different from the way it is in the rest of the passage?

Ⓐ Alice's world is more realistic in the first two paragraphs.

Ⓑ Alice's world is more interesting in the first two paragraphs.

Ⓒ Alice's world is less believable in the first two paragraphs.

Ⓓ Alice's world is less colorful in the first two paragraphs.

4. Read this sentence from the passage:

> Alice started to her feet, for it flashed across her mind that she had never before seen a rabbit with either a waistcoat-pocket, or a watch to take out of it, and burning with curiosity, she ran across the field after it, and fortunately was just in time to see it pop down a large rabbit-hole under the hedge.

In this sentence, "burning with curiosity" means that Alice was very

Ⓐ hot

Ⓑ sick

Ⓒ interested

Ⓓ angry

5. What does the picture show about the story?

Ⓐ It shows that rabbits are like people.

Ⓑ It shows how strange its events are.

Ⓒ It shows how a waistcoat looks.

Ⓓ It shows that the rabbit is late.

Questions 6-10 pertain to the following passages:

The Woman Who Made a Wizard

In 1998, a new writer named J. K. Rowling amazed parents and teachers alike by inspiring young people to read. She did this with the help of a young wizard named Harry Potter. Rowling's book *Harry Potter and the Philosopher's Stone* was just the first in a series that would capture the world's imagination.

Joanne Rowling was born in Glouchester, England, in 1965. In the 1990s, she was a mother dreaming of a career as a writer. However, she was not able to get any of her stories published. Then one day while riding a train, she got an idea. She imagined a boy who seemed ordinary in every way. Little did he know he had powers that were anything but ordinary. In fact, little Harry Potter had such amazing powers that he was already famous in the world of his fellow wizards. Suddenly, this "normal" boy is thrown into a series of incredible adventures. He faces all kinds of creatures, villains, and dangerous situations, while making some loyal new friends along the way.

Although it was long, *Harry Potter and the Philosopher's Stone* became a major hit with young readers. They could not wait to find out what Harry did next. J. K. Rowling did not make them wait long. She published *Harry Potter and the Chamber of Secrets* just a year after her first book. Once again, the book was a success, and Rowling followed the sequel with five more in the series.

In 2007, J. K. Rowling published her final Harry Potter book, *Harry Potter and the Deathly Hallows*. By this point, both Harry and the readers who loved him had grown up. Rowling was ready to move on too, announcing plans to not only write more children's books, but ones for adults, as well. No matter what J. K. Rowling does next, she will always have many, many fans grateful that she created the most famous little wizard in modern literature.

From the Pages to the Screen

J. K. Rowling became one of the most popular writers in the world when she created a wizard named Harry Potter. The seven novels in her series sold millions of copies. So it was no great surprise when she was offered the chance to bring her wizard from the pages of her books to movie screens.

Harry Potter and the Philosopher's Stone had been in print for little over a year when Warner Bros. films bought the rights to make it into a movie. J. K. Rowling had great control over the movie. Since her book was set in England, she made sure the movie was filmed and set there, too. She also insisted that all of the actors were British, and young Daniel Radcliffe was chosen to play Harry. Rowling worked closely with the actors, telling them things about their characters *Harry Potter* readers didn't even know yet.

J. K. Rowling's work helped make the movie version of *Harry Potter and the Philosopher's Stone* the big success it was when it came out in 2001. Although its title was changed to *Harry Potter and the Sorcerer's Stone*, the story was still true to the one she created in her first *Harry Potter* book. Audiences loved the movie just as much as readers loved the book, and each new *Harry Potter* book received its own movie version. The final movie, *Harry Potter and the Deathly Hallows*, was released in two parts in 2010 and 2011. With that, the *Harry Potter* series came to an end. But that wonderful wizard continues to be just as popular as ever.

6. Read the sentence from the second passage:

J. K. Rowling became one of the most popular writers in the world when she created a wizard named Harry Potter.

Which sentence from the passage supports the idea that J. K. Rowling was "one of the most popular writers in the world"?

Ⓐ The seven novels in her series sold millions of copies.

Ⓑ J. K. Rowling had great control over the movie.

Ⓒ With that, the *Harry Potter* series came to an end.

Ⓓ They could not wait to find out what Harry did next.

7. What would you know if you read only both passages?

Ⓐ Both the *Harry Potter* books and the movies take place in England.

Ⓑ Harry Potter was a character in both books and movies.

Ⓒ The *Harry Potter* books ended in 2007, and the movies ended in 2011.

Ⓓ Audiences loved the *Harry Potter* books and the *Harry Potter* movies.

8. How were the *Harry Potter* books and the *Harry Potter* movies similar?

Ⓐ They both came out in 1998.

Ⓑ They both starred Daniel Radcliffe.

Ⓒ They both had final chapters released in two parts.

Ⓓ They both were very popular.

9. How are both passages organized?

Ⓐ Compare and contrast

Ⓑ Cause and effect

Ⓒ Problem and solution

Ⓓ Order of events

10. How is the first passage different from the second one?

Ⓐ The first passage is about a person, and the second one is about movies.

Ⓑ The first passage is about a wizard, and the second one is about a writer.

Ⓒ The first passage is about England, and the second one is about America.

Ⓓ The first passage is about *Harry Potter*, and the second one is about Daniel Radcliffe.

Questions 11-14 pertain to the following poem:

"My Shadow"
by Robert Louis Stevenson

I have a little shadow that goes in and out with me,
And what can be the use of him is more than I can see.
He is very, very like me from the heels up to the head;
And I see him jump before me, when I jump into my bed.

The funniest thing about him is the way he likes to grow—
Not at all like proper children, which is always very slow;
For he sometimes shoots up taller like an india-rubber ball,
And he sometimes gets so little that there's none of him at all.

He hasn't got a notion of how children ought to play,
And can only make a fool of me in every sort of way.
He stays so close beside me, he's a coward, you can see;
I'd think shame to stick to nursie as that shadow sticks to me!

One morning, very early, before the sun was up,
I rose and found the shining dew on every buttercup;
But my lazy little shadow, like an arrant sleepy-head,
Had stayed at home behind me and was fast asleep in bed.

11. The narrator intends the poem to be

Ⓐ funny

Ⓑ scary

Ⓒ sad

Ⓓ hopeful

12. What happens in the poem that cannot happen in real life?

Ⓐ The child's shadow does everything he does.

Ⓑ The child's shadow stays behind him in bed.

Ⓒ The child's shadow changes shape.

Ⓓ The child's shadow stays behind him.

13. What is the narrator saying about his shadow in the second verse?

Ⓐ It changes shape in different lights.

Ⓑ It is not like other shadows.

Ⓒ It looks like it is made of rubber.

Ⓓ It is not really his shadow.

14. Read this line from the poem:

He hasn't got a notion of how children ought to play

How is the gh pronounced in the word "ought"?

Ⓐ It is a *g* sound, as in "ghost."

Ⓑ It is an *f* sound, as in "paragraph."

Ⓒ It is a *g* sound, as in "germ."

Ⓓ It is silent.

15. Which sentence is the best way to begin an essay about Mount Rushmore?

Ⓐ George Washington is one of the presidents shown on Mount Rushmore.

Ⓑ Mount Rushmore is one of the biggest and most famous sculptures in America.

Ⓒ Each head on Mount Rushmore is about 60 feet tall.

Ⓓ Work on Mount Rushmore started in 1927.

16. Read the sentences:

It was raining outside. I brought an umbrella.

What is the best way to rewrite the second sentence?

Ⓐ Consequently, I brought an umbrella.

Ⓑ Specifically, I brought an umbrella.

Ⓒ Suddenly, I brought an umbrella.

Ⓓ Although I brought an umbrella.

17. What is the best way to end an essay about swimming?

Ⓐ It is important to have an adult around when you're learning to swim.

Ⓑ One way of swimming is called the backstroke.

Ⓒ Because it is so healthy and fun, I think swimming is the most important activity you can learn.

Ⓓ New swimmers should practice in water that is not so deep that it is over their heads.

18. Which sentence would be best in an essay about turtles?

Ⓐ Turtles are reptiles.

Ⓑ Turtles are reptiles, which means they lay eggs like birds.

Ⓒ Turtles are just like birds.

Ⓓ Turtles are animals and all animals take care of baby animals.

19. In an essay about Abraham Lincoln, which sentence best supports the claim that he thought people were only as happy as they wanted to be?

Ⓐ Abraham Lincoln probably always had a smile on his face, so he was probably always happy.

Ⓑ Abraham Lincoln thought people were usually happy.

Ⓒ As Abraham Lincoln once said, "Most folks are about as happy as they make their minds to be."

Ⓓ Sometimes Abraham Lincoln was very sad.

20. What is the best way to let the reader know a story is supposed to be funny?

Ⓐ Begin the story with a famous saying.

Ⓑ Begin the story by explaining that it is funny.

Ⓒ Begin the story with "Once upon a time."

Ⓓ Begin the story with a joke.

21. Which line from a story shows that the plot has changed?

Ⓐ Suddenly, Brett felt happier than he ever had in his life.

Ⓑ The winter morning was cold.

Ⓒ Trees surrounded the little house on the hill.

Ⓓ The dog was sleeping underneath the warm sun.

22. Read the sentences:

Sandra read the book. Sandra wrote a report about it.

What is the best way to combine these two sentences into a single one?

Ⓐ Sandra read the book, Sandra wrote a report about it.

Ⓑ Sandra read the book, then she wrote a report about it.

Ⓒ Sandra read the book, she wrote a report about it.

Ⓓ Sandra read the book wrote a report about it.

23. Read the sentences:

I like jogging. I mainly like jogging with a friend.

What is the best way to combine these two sentences into a single one?

Ⓐ I like jogging, and I mainly like jogging with a friend.

Ⓑ I like jogging, I mainly like jogging with a friend.

Ⓒ I like jogging with a friend.

Ⓓ I like jogging, especially with a friend.

24. Which is the best way to describe trees?

Ⓐ There were some trees.

Ⓑ The thick patch of green trees swayed in the breeze gently.

Ⓒ The trees were moving in the breeze.

Ⓓ All of the trees were coming out of the ground.

25. What is the best ending to a story about a girl searching for a missing dog?

Ⓐ The girl drinks milk.

Ⓑ The girl sees a cat.

Ⓒ The girl goes ice-skating.

Ⓓ The girl finds her dog.

26. Read the sentence:

Apu skipped through the front door and head off to school.

What is the best way to rewrite this sentence?

Ⓐ Apu skipped through the front door and headed off school.

Ⓑ Apu skipped through the front door, head off to school.

Ⓒ Apu skipped through the front door and headed off to school.

Ⓓ Leave it as is.

27. What is the best place to find facts for an essay on California?

Ⓐ A short story about California

Ⓑ A book by a writer from California

Ⓒ California's official website

Ⓓ A map of California

28. When using facts from books in an essay, you should

Ⓐ list the books you used at the end of the essay

Ⓑ change the way the facts are worded

Ⓒ read only the facts you need for your essay

Ⓓ copy entire paragraphs into your essay

29. Which is most important to do before a lesson about the book *Treasure Island*?

Ⓐ Read everything you can about the author of *Treasure Island*.

Ⓑ Read other books about pirates.

Ⓒ Watch the movie version of *Treasure Island*.

Ⓓ Write down any questions you might have about the book.

30. Which is the best question to ask during a lesson about the book *The Secret Garden*?

Ⓐ What is your favorite book by the author of *The Secret Garden*?

Ⓑ Why do the children work on the garden in the book?

Ⓒ How old were you when you first read *The Secret Garden*?

Ⓓ Why do we have to read books?

31. What should you not do while describing a story out loud?

Ⓐ Mention the main characters.

Ⓑ Describe the most important events in the story.

Ⓒ Explain how you would change the story.

Ⓓ Tell where the story takes place.

32. What is the best detail to include in an oral report about the history of airplanes?

Ⓐ Airplanes would be better if they could carry more people.

Ⓑ I first rode in an airplane when I was six years old.

Ⓒ Airplanes make too much noise.

Ⓓ The Wright brothers flew the first airplane in 1903.

33. What is the best way to change an oral report if you are giving it to very young children?

Ⓐ Change any difficult words to simpler ones.

Ⓑ Change all the adults in your report to children.

Ⓒ Include stories about things young children like.

Ⓓ Include the names of the children in your report.

34. Read the sentence:

The mouse ran under the table.

What does the word "under" show in this sentence?

Ⓐ It shows where the mouse lives.

Ⓑ It shows why the mouse ran.

Ⓒ It shows how the mouse ran.

Ⓓ It shows where the mouse ran.

35. Read the sentence:

We are going to ________the movies or the park this Saturday.

Which word best completes the sentence?

Ⓐ neither

Ⓑ either

Ⓒ nor

Ⓓ and

36. Read the sentence:

When Johnny was young, he ______ on Elm Street.

Which word completes the sentence best?

Ⓐ lives

Ⓑ live

Ⓒ lived

Ⓓ living

37. What is the best way to write the book title?

Ⓐ *Oliver Twist*

Ⓑ "Oliver Twist"

Ⓒ Oliver "Twist"

Ⓓ Oliver Twist

38. Read the sentences:

The horse ran through the field. It was tan.

What is the best way to rewrite these sentences?

Ⓐ The horse ran. Through the field. It was tan.

Ⓑ It was tan. The horse ran through the field.

Ⓒ The horse ran tan through the field.

Ⓓ The horse ran through the tan field.

39. Read the sentence:

Although the salad was not very good, the soup was <u>terrific</u>.

What does the word <u>terrific</u> mean?

Ⓐ Small

Ⓑ Hot

Ⓒ Bad

Ⓓ Great

40. What is the best way to write the sentence?

Ⓐ In 2008 my family moved to this town.

Ⓑ In 2008, my family moved to this town.

Ⓒ In 2008, my family moved, to this town.

Ⓓ In 2008 my family moved, to this town.

41. Read the dictionary entry:

increase [v. *in-krees*]
1. to become greater in size
2. to multiply

Which part of the entry shows you how to say the word?

Ⓐ increase

Ⓑ v.

Ⓒ *in-krees*

Ⓓ 1. to become greater in size

42. Read the sentence:

Sheila was head over heels when she received a puppy for her birthday.

What does "head over heels" mean in this sentence?

Ⓐ Very excited

Ⓑ Clumsy

Ⓒ Very confused

Ⓓ Slippery

43. Read the sentence:

Jose was planning to play baseball today; ________, it rained all day so he could not.

Which word completes the sentence best?

Ⓐ although

Ⓑ however

Ⓒ similarly

Ⓓ in addition

44. Read the sentence

By the end of today, I __________ two miles.

Ⓐ will have walked

Ⓑ had walked

Ⓒ have walked

Ⓓ walked

45. What is the best way to write the sentence?

Ⓐ Last Monday we had class outside because it is so sunny.

Ⓑ Last Monday we have class outside because it was so sunny.

Ⓒ Last Monday we had class outside because it will be so sunny.

Ⓓ Last Monday we had class outside because it was so sunny.

46. Which word is spelled correctly?

Ⓐ Midnite

Ⓑ Kingdum

Ⓒ Familiar

Ⓓ Handkercheif

Practice Test #2

Practice Questions

Questions 1-5 pertain to the following excerpt from Black Beauty: The Autobiography of a Horse by Anna Sewell:

Chapter 1 My Early Home

The first place that I can well remember was a large pleasant meadow with a pond of clear water in it. Some shady trees leaned over it, and rushes and water-lilies grew at the deep end. Over the hedge on one side we looked into a plowed field, and on the other we looked over a gate at our master's house, which stood by the roadside; at the top of the meadow was a grove of fir trees, and at the bottom a running brook overhung by a steep bank.

While I was young I lived upon my mother's milk, as I could not eat grass. In the daytime I ran by her side, and at night I lay down close by her. When it was hot we used to stand by the pond in the shade of the trees, and when it was cold we had a nice warm shed near the grove.

As soon as I was old enough to eat grass my mother used to go out to work in the daytime, and come back in the evening.

There were six young colts in the meadow besides me; they were older than I was; some were nearly as large as grown-up horses. I used to run with them, and had great fun; we used to gallop all together round and round the field as hard as we could go. Sometimes we had rather rough play, for they would frequently bite and kick as well as gallop.

One day, when there was a good deal of kicking, my mother whinnied to me to come to her, and then she said:

"I wish you to pay attention to what I am going to say to you. The colts who live here are very good colts, but they are cart-horse colts, and of course they have not learned manners. You have been well-bred and well-born; your father has a great name in these parts, and your grandfather won the cup two years at the Newmarket races; your grandmother had the sweetest temper of any horse I ever knew, and I think you have never seen me kick or bite. I hope you will grow up gentle and good, and never learn bad ways; do your work with a good will, lift your feet up well when you trot, and never bite or kick even in play."

I have never forgotten my mother's advice; I knew she was a wise old horse, and our master thought a great deal of her. Her name was Duchess, but he often called her Pet.

1. Which answer best shows what happens in the passage?

Ⓐ A pleasant meadow contains trees, water-lilies, a plowed field, and a house.

Ⓑ A young horse grows up in a meadow where it lives with its wise mother.

Ⓒ A young horse plays with six colts, but sometimes the colts play too rough.

Ⓓ A horse is chosen to run in a race where it beats six colts that are older than it.

2. What is the horse's mother's name?

Ⓐ Newmarket

Ⓑ Colt

Ⓒ Lily

Ⓓ Duchess

3. Read this sentence from the passage:

When it was hot we used to stand by the pond in the shade of the trees, and when it was cold we had a nice warm shed near the grove.

What does the word grove mean?

Ⓐ A very large house

Ⓑ A cool winter night

Ⓒ A patch of trees

Ⓓ A group of horses

4. Why does the horse think his mother is "wise"?

Ⓐ She knows the colts in the meadow are "cart-horse colts."

Ⓑ She gives him good advice about growing up gentle.

Ⓒ She has a master who likes to call her Pet.

Ⓓ She likes to kick and bite.

5. Read this paragraph from *The Call of the Wild*, a book about a dog named Buck:

Buck did not read the newspapers, or he would have known that trouble was brewing, not alone for himself, but for every tide-water dog, strong of muscle and with warm, long hair, from Puget Sound to San Diego. Because men, groping in the Arctic darkness, had found a yellow metal, and because steamship and transportation companies were booming the find, thousands of men were rushing into the Northland. These men wanted dogs, and the dogs they wanted were heavy dogs, with strong muscles by which to toil, and furry coats to protect them from the frost.

How is *Black Beauty* different from *The Call of the Wild*?

Ⓐ The animal in *Black Beauty* tells its own story.

Ⓑ *Black Beauty* is written for older readers.

Ⓒ There is no animal in *Black Beauty*.

Ⓓ *Black Beauty* is about a dog.

Questions 6-10 pertain to the following passage:

A Dreamer Named George Lucas

You may not know the name George Lucas, but you probably know the incredible world he created. He is the mastermind behind such beloved heroes as Luke Skywalker, R2D2, Chewbacca, and Queen Amidala. He also created such dreaded villains as Darth Vader, Boba Fett, and Emperor Palpatine. These are some of the main characters in the wildly popular series of movies called *Star Wars*. And none of these films would exist if not for a young dreamer from Modesto, California.

George Lucas was born on May 14, 1944. As a young man, George love driving his car around Modesto and dreamed of becoming a racecar driver. However, he became interested in film while studying at junior college. He focused on film while at the University of Southern California School of Cinematic Arts, where he learned the skills that would make him famous.

At the university, George made his first film. It was a science-fiction story called *THX 1138*. A friend of his thought the film was very serious. He challenged George to make a lighthearted comedy. George rose to the challenge by making a movie called *American Graffiti*. The movie was about a group of teenagers who liked nothing better than driving around town in their cars. The story was not very dramatic. The movie studio was concerned that people would not be very interested in his film. But audiences really related to the funny, likable characters, and the film became a big hit. George's success with *American Graffiti* meant he would be able to make more films.

For his next project, he returned to science fiction. But instead of making another serious, adult film like *THX 1138*, he decided to make one with the lighthearted, fast-paced feel of *American Graffiti*. Once again, the studio executives were worried that audiences would not like George's space adventure. They thought his world of creatures and robots was too strange. Once again, the studio was wrong. Released in 1977, *Star Wars* made more money than any movie before it. George was right again.

George Lucas spent the next few years working on sequels to his big hit. *Empire Strikes Back* was released in 1980. *Return of the Jedi* followed in 1983. In the meantime, he created a new character, an adventurer named Indiana Jones. Indiana would star in three popular movies of his own. It seemed that George could only have success, but making all of these films was a lot of hard work. He decided to take some time off from making movies, although he promised fans that there were more stories to tell in the *Star Wars* universe.

Sixteen years later, George Lucas finally returned to the most successful series in movie history. But instead of picking up where *Return of the Jedi* ended, he decided to tell the story of what happened before the first *Star Wars* movie he made. *The Phantom Menace* was released in 1999. Then came *Attack of the Clones* in 2002 and *Revenge of the Sith* in 2005.

When he isn't making blockbusters, George Lucas likes to spend time with his family. He even allowed his three children to appear in his most recent *Star Wars* movies. Who knows what he will dream up next?

6. Which line from the passage shows that some people were not sure if George would be a success?

Ⓐ George's success with *American Graffiti* meant he would be able to make more films.

Ⓑ The movie studio was concerned that people would not be very interested in his film.

Ⓒ Indiana would star in three popular movies of his own.

Ⓓ A friend of his thought the film was very serious.

7. Which answer best shows what happens in the passage?

Ⓐ A boy from Modesto, California, grew up to be a successful moviemaker.

Ⓑ George Lucas started making his first *Star Wars* movies in 1999.

Ⓒ A boy liked racecars when he was young, but he studied moviemaking in college.

Ⓓ A young movie fan grows up to be a successful racecar driver.

8. How are the Indiana Jones movies similar to the *Star Wars* movies?

Ⓐ They both take place in space.

Ⓑ They both began in 1977.

Ⓒ They are both about racecars.

Ⓓ They are both adventures.

9. Read the sentence from the passage:

He is the mastermind behind such <u>beloved</u> heroes as Luke Skywalker, R2D2, Chewbacca, and Queen Amidala.

What does <u>beloved</u> mean?

Ⓐ Scary

Ⓑ Unknown

Ⓒ Popular

Ⓓ Hated

10. What is the name of George Lucas's first movie?

Ⓐ *THX 1138*

Ⓑ *American Graffiti*

Ⓒ *The Empire Strikes Back*

Ⓓ *The Phantom Menace*

Questions 11-14 pertain to the following poem:

"Little White Lily"
by George Macdonald

Little White Lily
Sat by a stone,
Drooping and waiting
Till the sun shone.
Little White Lily
Sunshine has fed;
Little White Lily
Is lifting her head.

Little White Lily
Said: "It is good
Little White Lily's
Clothing and food."
Little White Lily

Dressed like a bride!
Shining with whiteness,
And crownèd beside!

Little White Lily
Drooping with pain,
Waiting and waiting
For the wet rain.
Little White Lily
Holdeth her cup;
Rain is fast falling
And filling it up.

Little White Lily
Said: "Good again,
When I am thirsty
To have the nice rain.
Now I am stronger,
Now I am cool;
Heat cannot burn me,
My veins are so full."

Little White Lily
Smells very sweet;
On her head sunshine,
Rain at her feet.
Thanks to the sunshine,
Thanks to the rain,
Little White Lily
Is happy again.

11. How is the poem organized?

Ⓐ Each verse includes something that Little White Lily says.

Ⓑ Each verse explains how Little White Lily spends every day of the week.

Ⓒ Each verse describes something different that Little White Lily does.

Ⓓ Each verse proves that Little White Lily is always happy.

12. This poem is about a

Ⓐ girl

Ⓑ raindrop

Ⓒ stone

Ⓓ flower

13. Read these lines from the poem:

Little White Lily
Dressed like a bride!

These lines mean that Little White Lily is

Ⓐ white

Ⓑ wearing a dress

Ⓒ married

Ⓓ an adult

14. What makes Little White Lily stop drooping in the first verse?

Ⓐ The rain

Ⓑ The sun

Ⓒ A crown

Ⓓ A cup

15. Which sentence would best begin an essay about farming?

Ⓐ Some farmers grow only one thing, like strawberries.

Ⓑ Farmers plant seeds in soil and take care of them to help them grow.

Ⓒ People all over the world need the fruits and vegetables that grow on farms.

Ⓓ If was on a farm I'd do farming like vegetables.

16. Which sentence would best end an essay about drawing?

Ⓐ Other forms of art are sculpting, painting, and collage.

Ⓑ There is a picture of an old schoolhouse hanging in the museum.

Ⓒ As I have shown, drawing is not only fun but it is a great way to express yourself.

Ⓓ Crayons can be melted down and shaped into all kinds of figures.

17. When preparing to write an essay about bears, it is important to

Ⓐ write your notes as quickly as possible

Ⓑ make up some stories about bears

Ⓒ draw some pictures of bears

Ⓓ read more than one book about bears

18. What is the best sentence to include in an essay about why trees are important?

Ⓐ Trees give off oxygen, which helps people to breathe.

Ⓑ Trees can grow very tall or be pretty small.

Ⓒ You can build a tree house in a tree.

Ⓓ I think trees are really pretty.

19. What would be important to do in an essay about life during the 1700s and life today?

Ⓐ Prove that life has not changed.

Ⓑ Create characters to tell the stories.

Ⓒ Explain how they are different.

Ⓓ Show that life can be a lot of fun.

20. Read this sentence from an essay about exercise:

Doctors agree that exercise is important to being healthy.

Why does the writer mention doctors in this sentence?

Ⓐ To prove that the writer has read some books about exercise

Ⓑ To support the idea that exercise is important to being healthy

Ⓒ To explain how doctors do their jobs

Ⓓ To show that people who do not exercise are never healthy

21. Read the sentences:

Some people travel only by bicycle. Some people drive cars.

What is the best way to combine these two sentences into a single one?

Ⓐ Some people travel only by bicycle, some people drive cars.

Ⓑ Some people travel only by bicycle and car.

Ⓒ Some people travel only by bicycle, and they are different from some people who drive cars.

Ⓓ Some people only travel by bicycle in contrast to people who drive cars.

22. Which is the best sentence to include in an essay about Benjamin Franklin?

Ⓐ Benjamin Franklin is on the $100 bill, and George Washington is on the $1 bill.

Ⓑ Benjamin Franklin was one of the Founding Fathers of the United States.

Ⓒ My uncle looks a lot like Benjamin Franklin.

Ⓓ There was a show about Benjamin Franklin on television last night.

23. Read the sentences:

Petra read the book. Greg read the book first.

What is the best way to combine these two sentences into a single one?

Ⓐ Petra read the book after Greg.

Ⓑ Petra read the book, Greg read the book first.

Ⓒ Petra read the book, then Greg read the book.

Ⓓ Greg read the book, but Petra read it first.

24. Read the sentences:

Bob loves movies. Funny ones are his favorites.

What is the best way to rewrite the second sentence?

Ⓐ Consequently, funny ones are his favorites.

Ⓑ Strangely, funny ones are his favorites.

Ⓒ Specifically, funny ones are his favorites.

Ⓓ Surely, funny ones are his favorites.

25. Read this sentence from a story:

Eliza trembled like a leaf when she heard the strange noise coming from the woods.

This sentence shows that Eliza is

Ⓐ cold

Ⓑ tired

Ⓒ happy

Ⓓ scared

26. Which is the best way to describe snow?

Ⓐ Snow is white.

Ⓑ There was snow all over the place.

Ⓒ The kids played in the snow all day.

Ⓓ The fresh white flakes of snow drifted to the ground slowly.

27. What is the best way to improve your writing?

Ⓐ Write one new sentence every week.

Ⓑ Try writing on different types of paper.

Ⓒ Write in a journal every day.

Ⓓ Write with a pencil instead of on a computer.

28. What is the best thing to do before writing an essay on healthy eating?

Ⓐ Write a short story about eating healthy.

Ⓑ Read a few books about healthy eating.

Ⓒ Eat a lot of fruits and vegetables.

Ⓓ Visit a farm.

29. If the teacher asks a question you would like to answer, you should

Ⓐ write down your answer and save it for a later time

Ⓑ give your answer before the teacher has finished asking the question

Ⓒ shout out your answer as loud as you can

Ⓓ raise your hand and wait for your teacher to call on you

30. What is the best way to remember the main ideas from a lesson?

Ⓐ Ask a lot of questions during the lesson.

Ⓑ Take notes during the lesson.

Ⓒ Do your best to remember the main ideas.

Ⓓ Do your homework after the lesson.

31. Which is the most important thing to include in an oral report about bees?

Ⓐ A quotation from a book about bees

Ⓑ A story about a bee you once saw

Ⓒ A lesson about other flying insects

Ⓓ An imitation of a bee's buzz

32. When might it be proper to play music in class?

Ⓐ During a math lesson

Ⓑ When giving a report about music

Ⓒ While having quiet study time

Ⓓ When asking questions during a lesson

33. What is the best detail to include in an oral report about monkeys?

Ⓐ I love monkeys.

Ⓑ Cats and monkeys both climb trees.

Ⓒ There are about 260 different kinds of monkeys.

Ⓓ My cousin likes to draw pictures of monkeys.

34. What is the best way to write the sentence?

Ⓐ Are you coming with me Julie?

Ⓑ Are you, coming with me Julie?

Ⓒ Are you coming with, me Julie?

Ⓓ Are you coming with me, Julie?

35. What is the best way to write the sentence?

Ⓐ He will buy apples, peaches, bananas, and pears at the store.

Ⓑ He will buy apples peaches, bananas, and pears at the store.

Ⓒ He will buy apples, peaches bananas and pears at the store.

Ⓓ He will buy apples peaches bananas and pears at the store.

36. The word "homophone" means

Ⓐ look alike

Ⓑ telephone

Ⓒ sound alike

Ⓓ home

37. Read the sentences:

The snowy meadow was as pretty as a picture.

What does this sentence mean?

Ⓐ There is a picture of a meadow.

Ⓑ Meadows are difficult to draw.

Ⓒ Snow makes meadows look like pictures.

Ⓓ The meadow looks nice.

38. Read the sentence:

Tina used to be happy, but now she is <u>furious</u>.

What does <u>furious</u> mean?

Ⓐ Glad

Ⓑ Angry

Ⓒ Strong

Ⓓ Brave

39. Read these lines from a story:

"Goodbye, Candace," Bill and Serena said while waving to their friend.

"Y'all come and visit me in Georgia anytime!" Candace replied.

Why does the writer use the word "y'all" in this story?

Ⓐ The writer does not know how to spell.

Ⓑ The writer is too lazy to write out "you all."

Ⓒ The writer is showing how some people in Georgia speak.

Ⓓ The writer thinks it is funny to make up new words.

40. Read the sentence:

Before tomorrow, I __________ the book.

Which word best completes the sentence?

Ⓐ read

Ⓑ will have read

Ⓒ have read

Ⓓ had read

41. Read the sentence:

Maurice turned off the lamp because it was too bright and light.

What is the best way to rewrite this sentence?

Ⓐ Maurice turned off the lamp because it was too bright.

Ⓑ Maurice turned off the lamp because it was too light and bright.

Ⓒ Maurice turned off the lamp because it was too.

Ⓓ Maurice turned off the lamp because it was too bright, light, and shiny.

42. What is the best way to write the song title?

Ⓐ I Want to Hold Your Hand

Ⓑ <u>I Want to Hold Your Hand</u>

Ⓒ *I Want to Hold Your Hand*

Ⓓ "I Want to Hold Your Hand"

43. Read the sentences:

Pete plays the guitar. ____________, Keith plays the drums.

Which word best completes the second sentence?

Ⓐ Although

Ⓑ However

Ⓒ Similarly

Ⓓ In addition

44. Read the sentence:

Kris is washing the car while Lexi walked the dog.

What is the best way to rewrite this sentence?

Ⓐ Kris will wash the car while Lexi walked the dog.

Ⓑ Kris washed the car while Lexi walked the dog.

Ⓒ Kris had washed the car while Lexi walked the dog.

Ⓓ Kris washes the car while Lexi walked the dog.

45. Read the sentence:

The dog and cat are ______ on the rug.

Which word completes the sentence best?

Ⓐ sleep

Ⓑ slept

Ⓒ sleeps

Ⓓ sleeping

46. Read the sentence:

If you do not water the plant, it will <u>perish</u>.

What does the word <u>perish</u> mean?

Ⓐ Die

Ⓑ Live

Ⓒ Grow

Ⓓ Move

Thank You

We at Mometrix would like to extend our heartfelt thanks to you, our friend and patron, for allowing us to play a part in your journey. It is a privilege to serve people from all walks of life who are unified in their commitment to building the best future they can for themselves.

The preparation you devote to these important testing milestones may be the most valuable educational opportunity you have for making a real difference in your life. We encourage you to put your heart into it—that feeling of succeeding, overcoming, and yes, conquering will be well worth the hours you've invested.

We want to hear your story, your struggles and your successes, and if you see any opportunities for us to improve our materials so we can help others even more effectively in the future, please share that with us as well. **The team at Mometrix would be absolutely thrilled to hear from you!** So please, send us an email (support@mometrix.com) and let's stay in touch.

Online Resources

Due to our efforts to try to keep this book to a manageable length, we've created a link that will give you access to all of your online resources:

mometrix.com/resources719/ssmcag5readwb

It's Your Moment, Let's Celebrate It!

Share your story @mometrixtestpreparation

TABLE OF CONTENTS

Workbook Answers

Reading: Literature

Living on a Ranch

1. C - The Bar M Bar Ranch is in Laramie, Wyoming
2. D - Marcus uses whistles and calls.
3. B - Marcus enjoys working with the sheep.
4. A - Everyone has a job on a ranch.
5. C - She is in charge of the household and bills.
6. B - Working and living on a ranch is a full time job.
7. B - People who work on a ranch owned by someone else.
8. A - They all help with chores on the ranch.

Geocaching

1. C - He always has fun when he was with Tommy and Mr. Jones.
2. A - The GPS was only accurate to 15 feet.
3. C - wool socks, hiking boots, and a backpack
4. A - Geocaching is a treasure hunt for small containers using GPS coordinates.
5. B - small items or toys to trade
6. D - Yes, Tommy teaches Sam about marking off a search area.
7. B - two friends going Geocaching with Mr. Jones
8. D - a hiding place

Dance Class

1. A - They want to learn to dance.
2. C - Jillian loves ballet, and Samantha loves tap.
3. D - Both classrooms have wooden floors and mirrors.
4. C - a classical type of dance
5. D - a bar on the wall for stretching
6. B - how much the sisters loved dance

Island Ponies

1. C - Assateague horses and Chincoteague ponies are the same breed of horse.
2. B - someone who watches
3. D - They both have a National Park.
4. A - two herds of horses on Assateague Island
5. B - The Chincoteague ponies are given veterinary care.
6. D - The reader might think the firefighters were just being mean to the ponies.

Katie's Journal

1. A - Katie having a fight with her friend Sandy.
2. B - strained
3. C - The reader wouldn't know that the fight had been resolved.
4. A - The reader would not be able to know Katie's thoughts.
5. A - Katie was angry, but she became calm.
6. C - Even though they weren't speaking, Katie and Sandy still found a way to be mean in science.

An Artist Thinking BIG

1. D - Gutzon Borglum
2. A - Mount Rushmore is the most famous of the three mountain carvings.
3. B - All three carvings were finished by someone other than the original artist.
4. B - huge
5. A - three mountain carvings and the artist that connects them
6. D - Crazy Horse is the biggest and isn't finished yet.

The Disappearing Hair Ribbons

1. B - someone who is thought to be guilty
2. A - Pilar is upset.
3. B - Pilar's ribbons went missing before Rosa agreed to help.
4. A - Rosa searched Riley's habitat after she agreed to help.
5. A - Stinky climbed in Pilar's boot after Rosa agreed to help.
6. C - Pilar and Rosa were neighborhood detectives.

Reading: Informational

Animals of Yellowstone

1. D - He wanted to know where to look for the animals.
2. A - South Entrance and West Thumb
3. B - Elk
4. C - More animals live in forests and meadows.
5. D - an animal's home area
6. B - The wolves have the smallest population.

A Day in the City

1. D - subway
2. C - Which subway lines would you take to get to the National Archives?
3. B - They enjoy doing things together.
4. C - The White House and the National Air and Space Museum
5. A - Definition 1. - A sheet arranging information into columns or tabs
6. A - It is only on one subway line.

Family Names

1. C - to explain family names based on occupation
2. A - to move people or things
3. D - definitions and origins of occupational words
4. B - was a chef.
5. A - Fletcher and Bender
6. C - last Name

Meteor Watching

1. C - The Perseid meteor shower is a favorite.
2. A - It only happens in August.
3. C - scattered fragments of rock
4. D - The Earth takes one year to orbit the sun, and the comet takes 135 years to orbit the sun.

5. B - People enjoy watching the shower because it happens in the summer.
6. B - average

Reading: Foundational Skills

Root Words

1. cycle
2. comfort
3. bio
4. fill
5. arrange

Prefixes

1. *ir-* C: lacking responsibility
2. *anti-* B: a liquid used to keep other liquids from freezing
3. *im-* A: not able to occur
4. *mis-* D: an error
5. *pre-* B: before written records

Suffixes

1. *-ly;* A: in the right manner.
2. *-ful;* B: feeling or causing happiness
3. *-ist;* C: a person who studies science
4. *-ian;* D: a person who plays music
5. *-ment;* A: a feeling of eagerness

Language

Language Answer Key

Prepositions

1. between
2. over
3. across
4. toward
5. around

Conjunctions

1. and - coordinating
2. because - subordinating
3. Neither/nor - correlative
4. although - subordinating
5. not only / but also - correlative
6. but - subordinating
7. and - coordinating
8. Either / or - correlative
9. unless - subordinating
10. Both / and - correlative

Verb Tenses

1. will go - C
2. cooks - A
3. rained - B
4. will visit - C
5. lives - A
6. rode
7. enjoys
8. will read
9. wanted
10. will play

Capitalization

1. Yes
2. Yes
3. No
4. Yes
5. Yes
6. No
7. Yes
8. Yes

Ending Punctuation

1. Question mark (?)
2. Period (.)
3. Period (.)
4. Exclamation point (!)
5. Question mark (?)
6. Exclamation point (!)
7. Question mark (?)
8. Period (.)
9. Question mark (?)
10. Exclamation point (!)

Commas

1. In Houston, Texas, there is a huge rodeo in February.
2. Johnny said, "Let's go play on the swings."
3. It's going to rain today, isn't it?
4. Nate had three apples, two oranges, and a banana in his lunch box.
5. Eureka, a show on the SyFy channel, is about a town of geniuses.
6. The Revolutionary War officially ended on May 12, 1784.
7. Yes, thank you, I would love some cake.
8. Along with his friends, Evan thought he could help others.
9. Because of the lightning, we could not play outside.
10. We can vacation at the beach, or we can go to the city.

11. & 12. Answers will vary

Titles

1. <u>To Kill A Mockingbird</u> is my favorite novel.
2. The headline read, "Man Kills Seven in Subway."
3. My class went to see "An Ideal Husband," a play by Oscar Wilde.
4. <u>The Avengers</u> was the best movie this summer!
5. "What Sarah Said," by Death Cab for Cutie, is the best song ever.

Changing Sentences

1. Nate and Evan go to the Houston Zoo on Sundays.
2. Dragonflies live by the river, where I hope to see some today.
3. Evan likes the monkeys that live in the primate habitat.
4. Baboons are from African and Asia, but they mostly live in zoos now.
5. Nick watches the baby giraffe as it tries to eat leaves from a tall tree.

Homophones

1. two
2. right
3. there
4. one
5. threw
6. err
7. aisle
8. ate
9. bass
10. bare

Heteronyms

1. The Polish furniture needs <u>polish</u>. (a substance to give a shiny surface)
2. I <u>object</u> to that object. (disapprove)
3. She was too close to the window to <u>close</u> it. (to shut)
4. The bass drum had a <u>bass</u> painted on it. (a fish)
5. Mr. Jones is ready to <u>present</u> the present to the President. (to give formally)
6. Don't <u>desert</u> us just because we are in the desert. (to leave)
7. The <u>dove</u> dove for the food. (a bird)

8. Give me a minute and I'll show you minute particles in my microscope. (tiny)
9. The Grateful Dead are here to record a new record. (to preserve in sound)
10. I refuse to take out the refuse. (to say no)

Greek / Latin

1. A. photogenic
   B. photograph
   C. telephoto
   D. photosynthesis

2. A. aerodynamics
   B. aerobics
   C. aerate
   D. aeronautics

3. A. epidemic
   B. democracy
   C. demographic
   D. endemic

Context Clues

1. A - moved
2. B - get rid of
3. D - denied
4. A - huge
5. C - calm

Reference Materials

1. B - (2) /ˈmin(ē)əCHər/
2. C - (3)adj. of a much smaller size than normal
   noun. a thing that is much smaller than normal
   verb. represent on a smaller scale

3. D - (4)synonyms: diminutive, tiny, small
4. A - (1) Min-i-a-ture

5. D - Encyclopedia
6. A - Dictionary
7. C - Thesaurus
8. B - Glossary

Figurative language
1. A - simile
2. D - onomatopoeia
3. E - idiom
4. B - metaphor
5. C - alliteration

Synonyms
1. big
2. hard
3. bucket
4. mad
5. talk

Antonyms
6. city
7. full
8. beautiful / pretty
9. thaw
10. catch

Practice Test Answers

Practice Test #1

Answers and Explanations

1. C: Alice hears the rabbit talk, which is something rabbits cannot do. But she did not "think it so very much out of the way." This means she did not think it was very strange.

2. D: Choice D shows what happens through the whole passage. Choice A shows what happens in only the first paragraph. Choice B shows what happens in only the sixth paragraph. Choice C does not happen in the passage at all.

3. A: In the first paragraph of the passage, Alice is just sitting next to her sister on a riverbank. There is nothing unusual about the rabbit when she first sees it at the end of the second paragraph. In the third paragraph, the rabbit begins talking. Then Alice follows it into a hole where strange things happen. Such new developments are not realistic.

4. C: The common phrase "burning with curiosity" means that someone is very interested in something. It does not mean someone is actually burning, so choice A is wrong.

5. B: The picture shows how strange the story is by giving you a clear idea of what Alice saw. A rabbit wearing clothes, standing like a person, and reading a watch is very strange indeed. The picture shows a rabbit that is a lot like a person, but this is not how rabbits really are. So choice A is wrong. The picture does show how a waistcoat looks, but this is not very important to the story. So choice C is wrong too. Choice D is wrong because simply reading a watch does not mean someone is late.

6. A: Only a very popular writer could sell millions of books. Choices B and C do not show that J. K. Rowling was very popular. Choice D is from the first passage, not the second one.

7. C: Only the first passage mentions that the *Harry Potter* books ended in 2007. Only the second passage mentions that the *Harry Potter* movies ended in 2011. But choices A, B, and D are all mentioned in the second passage.

8. B: Both the *Harry Potter* books and the *Harry Potter* movies were very popular. Choice A is wrong, because only the book first came out in 1998. An actor cannot star in a fictional book, so choice B is wrong. The first passage does not say that the final *Harry Potter* book was released in two parts, so choice C is wrong.

9. D: Both passages are organized in the order of when things happened. Choice A, compare and contrast, is where the writer points out the things that are similar and different about two or more things. Choice B, cause and effect, is where the writer shows how something caused something else to happen. Choice C, problem and solution, is where the writer introduces a problem and explains how it was solved.

10. A: The first passage is a biography of J. K. Rowling. A biography is the story of a person's life. The second passage is about the movies based on J. K. Rowling's books.

11. A: The narrator talks about his shadow as if it were a real person. He mentions all the fantastic things his shadow seems to do. This creates a silly, funny mood. Shadows can sometimes be used to create a scary mood, but this is not how they are used in this poem. So choice B is wrong.

12. B: A child's shadow cannot stay at home sleeping in bed after the child has left the home. The other answer choices describe things shadows can do in real life.

13. A: A shadow can grow bigger or shrink depending on the light around it. This is what the narrator is describing when he says it "sometimes shoots up taller like an india-rubber ball" and "sometimes gets so little that there's none of him at all."

14. D: The letters gh are silent in the word "ought." This means you do not pronounce them at all.

15. B: The first sentence of an essay should introduce the topic in a general way. Choice B does this well. Choices A, C, and D are details that should be included in an essay on Mount Rushmore, but they are not general enough to begin it.

16. A: The word "consequently" is used to show cause and result. Because it was raining, the result was that the person brought an umbrella. Choice B, "Specifically," is used to narrow down a general idea. Choice C, "Suddenly," is used to show that something happened very fast and without warning. Choice D, "Although," is used to show that something happened in spite of what came before it.

17. C: The final sentence in an essay should sum up the essay's most important points. Choice C does this well. Choices A, B, and D are details that should be included in an essay on swimming, but they are not general enough to end it.

18. B: A good essay uses exact details to make its information clear. Choice B gives clear information about turtles by explaining what they are (reptiles) and a fact about reptiles ("they lay eggs") supported with a description of that fact ("like birds"). The other answer choices are not as clear or detailed.

19. C: Quotes are great ways to support information in an essay. This quote from Abraham Lincoln shows exactly how he felt about happiness. Choice A seems like the writer is making a guesses. You should never make guesses in an essay. Choice B needs more details to make it more exact.

20. D: The narrator's voice sets the mood of a story. By beginning a story with a joke, the reader will know that it is supposed to be funny. Explaining that it is funny is not a very clever or interesting way to let the reader know this. So choice B is wrong.

21. A: The word "Suddenly" is used to show that something unexpected is happening. The writer also says that Brett felt a way he never felt before in his life. These are clues that the plot is changing.

22. B: The word "then" shows that something happened after something else. Sandra wrote the report after reading the book. Choice B shows this most clearly.

23. D: The word "especially" is used to show the main way something is. By using it to link two ideas, you can avoid repeating information (choices A and B). Choice C just shows that the speaker likes jogging with a friend. It does not show that the speaker "mainly" likes jogging with a friend.

24. B: Choice B creates a clear picture of trees by using the describing words "thick," "green," and "gently." The word "swayed" also shows what they were doing.

25. D: The writer should solve the main problem by the end of a story. The main problem of this story is that the girl's dog is missing. The answer choice that solves this problem is choice D. Choices A, B, and C are all about things that have nothing to do with the missing dog.

26. C: Sometimes writing needs to be changed so that it is clear and correct. The original sentence needs to be changed. The first part of the sentence ("Apu skipped through the front door") is written in the past tense. The second part of the sentence ("and head off to school") is in the present tense. These parts need to be in the same tense. Choice C makes this change by changing "head" to "headed."

27. C: A lot of good facts can be found on the right websites. A state's official website is a good place to find facts about that state. Fiction writers sometimes change the facts to help their stories, so choice A is wrong. A writer who lives in California might not actually write about the state, so choice B is wrong. A map of California might give some information about where things are in the state, but it won't have as many facts as a website.

28. A: It is important to give credit to the books you used to research an essay. A list of sources at the end of the essay is a good way to do this.

29. D: A good way to prepare for a lesson on any topic is to write down any questions you might have about the topic. This will help get you involved in the lesson by giving you some things to ask. Articles about the author of a book (choice A) or the movie version of it (choice C) may not give you much information about the book.

30. B: During lessons, always ask questions that stay on topic. A question about a detail in the book is a good one to ask. Choices A and C are personal questions for the teacher that do not really focus on the book.

31. C: A good summary sticks to the most important details in a story. Characters (choice A), plot (choice B), and setting (choice D) are all important details. Choice C is wrong because your own ideas about how to change the story have nothing to do with what really happens in the story.

32. D: Be sure to always stay on topic when making an oral report. Choice D does this by giving an important fact about the history of airplanes. Choices A and C are opinions, not facts. Choice B is a detail about the speaker's own life. It has nothing to do with the topic.

33. A: The best speakers understand their audiences. Very young children may not know the same words you do, so it is smart to make the difficult ones simpler. This shows that you understand your audience. Choices B, C, and D are wrong because you should never change the facts in an oral report just to entertain your audience.

34. D: The word "under" is a preposition. Prepositions are words that show where things are.

35. B: The word "or" indicates things that might happen. The word "either" belongs with "or." The words "neither" and nor" indicate things that will not happen. So choices A and C are wrong. Choice D, "and," does not make any sense in this sentence.

36. C: The phrase "When Johnny was young" shows that this sentence takes place in the past. The past tense version of the verb "live" is "lived."

37. A: A book title needs to be written in slanted text called *italics.* Quotation marks are used for short stories, not books, so choice B is wrong.

38. D: Sometimes unclear sentences can be improved by combining them. The sentences in this question are unclear, because we do not know if the horse or the field is tan. Only choice D makes it clear that the field is tan.

39. D: Here's a clue: the word "although" is used to show that one thing is different from another. If the salad is not very good, the soup is different because it is great. You can use that clue to figure out that the word "terrific" means "great."

40. B: A comma should be used to separate a phrase that introduces a sentence from the rest of the sentence. The phrase "In 2008" introduces this sentence, and it needs to be separated with a comma.

41. C: A dictionary shows you how to say a word by sounding it out. Choice A is the word, but it does not show you exactly how to say it and what the syllables are. Only choice C does this.

42. A: The phrase "head over heels" is an idiom. An idiom is a phrase used to mean something other than it actually means. The phrase "head over heels" is commonly used to mean "very excited."

43. B: The word "however" is used to show a contrast. Jose planned to play baseball today. In contrast to that plan, he did not play because it rained all day.

44. A: This sentence is about something that is going to happen in the future. The correct way to show the future perfect tense is by using "will have."

45. D: This sentence takes place in the past ("Last Monday"). So all of its verbs should be written in the past tense. The only answer choice that uses two past tense verbs, "had" and "was," is choice D. Choice A contains the present tense verb "is." Choice B contains the present tense verb "have." Choice C contains the future tense verb phrase "will be."

46. C: Choice C, "familiar," is the only choice that is spelled correctly. Choice A should be spelled "midnight." Choice B should be spelled "kingdom." Choice D should be spelled "handkerchief."

Practice Test #2

Answer Key and Explanations

1. B: Choice B shows what happens through the whole passage. Choice A shows what happens in only the first paragraph. Choice C shows what happens in only the fourth paragraph. Choice D does not happen in the passage at all.

2. D: In the last paragraph of the passage, the horse says his mother's name is Duchess. Newmarket is the name of the race the horse's grandfather won, so choice A is wrong. A colt is a kind of horse, so choice B is wrong.

3. C: By rereading how the word "grove" is used in the passage, you can figure out that it means "a patch of trees."

4. B: Someone who is wise is smart and gives good advice. The horse knows his mother is wise because her advice about growing up gentle is good. Choices A and C are true, but they don't show that the horse's mother is wise. The horse's mother says "you have never seen me kick or bite," so choice D is wrong.

5. A: In *Black Beauty*, the horse tells or narrates its own story. In *The Call of the Wild*, an unnamed narrator tells Buck's story. *Black Beauty* is written in simpler language than *The Call of the Wild*. That means it is probably for younger readers, so choice B is wrong. Choices C and D are wrong because *Black Beauty* is about a horse.

6. B: Studio executives were afraid that George Lucas's movie *American Graffiti* might not be a success. They thought people would not be interested in the movie. His success as a moviemaker depended on the success of his movies.

7. B: Choice B shows what happens through the whole passage. Choice A shows what happens in only the fifth paragraph. Choice C shows what happens in only the second paragraph. Choice D does not happen in the passage at all.

8. D: The author calls *Star Wars* a space adventure in paragraph 4. In paragraph 5, the author calls the Indiana Jones movies adventures. So you can conclude that both the Indiana Jones and *Star Wars* movies are adventures.

9. C: People usually like heroes. They especially like heroes in successful movies. So you can guess that <u>beloved</u> means <u>popular</u>.

10. A: The third paragraph says that George Lucas's first movie was called *THX 1138*. He made *American Graffiti*, *The Empire Strikes Back*, and *The Phantom Menace* later in his career.

11. C: Each verse of the poem describes something different that Little White Lily does. There are quotations from Lily in two verses, but the other ones do not have quotations. So choice A is wrong. Little White Lily is in pain and weeping in the third verse, so choice D is wrong.

12. D: The poet makes Little White Lily seem like a girl. She talks, holds a cup, and feels happy. But the poet is really using images to describe a flower waiting for the sun and the rain.

13. A: Sometimes poets use words to mean something other than they seem to mean. They do this to make images with words. Little White Lily is not really wearing a dress (choice B). She just looks like a bride. Brides often wear white. So these lines mean that Little White Lily is white.

14. B: In the first verse, Little White Lily droops until "Sunshine has fed" her. Then she lifts her head, which means she has stopped drooping.

15. C: Choice C explains why farming is important. This is a clear and strong way to begin an essay on farming. Choices A and B might be details you would include in the middle of the essay. But they do not introduce the topic of farming well. Choice D is not written clearly.

16. C: An essay should end with a sentence that mentions the most important ideas that came before it. Choice C mentions two important ideas. It mentions that drawing is fun and that drawing is a great way to express yourself. This is a good way to end an essay about drawing. Choices A, B, and D stray from the topic of drawing to mention other things.

17. D: When preparing to write an essay on any topic, you should always read more than one book. This will give you more information about your topic.

18. A: Choice A says something important about trees. They help people to breathe. Choices B and C are not very important. Choice D is just an opinion about trees. It is not a reason they are important to everyone.

19. C: A good way to organize an essay about more than one thing is to explain how they are different. Life in the 1700s was very different from life today, so choice A is wrong. An essay should not contain made-up characters, so choice B is wrong.

20. B: Doctors know a lot about how to be healthy. The writer is giving some proof to support the idea that exercise is important to health by mentioning the opinions of health experts.

21. D: The phrase "in contrast" is used to show that one thing is different from another. It is a clear way to link two different ideas. Choice A is not a very good sentence because it repeats the phrase "some people." Choice B changes the meaning of the original sentences. Choice D is not written clearly.

22. B: Choice B mentions an important fact about Benjamin Franklin. Choice A strays from the topic by mentioning that George Washington is on the $1 bill. Choices C and D are not details about Benjamin Franklin's life. They do not belong in an essay about him.

23. A: Words such as "after" can be used to make the order of events clear. It shows that one thing happened, then another thing happened. Choice A is clear and written correctly. Choice B is wrong because it repeats the phrase "read the book." Choices C and D change the meaning of the original sentences.

24. C: The word "specifically" is used to narrow down an idea. The first sentence introduces a general idea ("Bob loves movies"). The second sentence narrows down the kind of movies Bob likes ("funny ones").

25. D: Authors use words to describe how a character feels without actually saying it. The word "strange" shows that something scary is happening. So you can guess that "Eliza trembled like a leaf" because she was "scared."

26. D: Choice D creates a clear picture of trees by using the describing words "fresh" and "white." It also shows what the snow did ("drifted to the ground") and how it did it ("slowly"). Choices A and B do not describe snow as well. Choice C does not describe snow at all. It just describes what the kids did in it.

27. C: The best way to improve your writing is to practice. Writing in a journal every day is a good way to practice writing. It is better than writing only once a week (choice A). The kind of paper you use (choice B) or the tool you use to write (choice D) will not make you a better writer.

28. B: Before writing any essay, always read some books to collect the facts you will include in the essay. Collecting facts is called research.

29. D: Different teachers have different rules for class discussions. But almost every teacher agrees that students should raise their hands when they want to speak in class.

30. B: The best way to remember the key ideas of a lesson is to write them down in your notebook. Then you can always study them later. Asking questions is good to do during a lesson, but it may not help you to remember the main ideas. So choice A is wrong. Your memory may not always be good enough to remember all the main ideas of a lesson, so choice C is wrong too.

31. A: You should always support the claims you make in a report. A good way to do this is to include a quotation from one of the books you used to write your report. This will prove that you are not just making up the details in it.

32. B: Some oral reports can be made better with different kinds of media, such as photos or music. While it would not be proper to play music during a math lesson, it might be proper to play it during a report about music. It is a way to give examples of what you are discussing.

33. C: Be sure to always stay on topic when making an oral report. Choice C does this by giving an important fact about monkeys. Choice A is an opinion, not a fact. Choice C strays off topic by mentioning cats. Choice D is a detail about the speaker's own life. It has nothing to do with the topic.

34. D: When a sentence is directed at a person, the person's name should be separated by a comma. Choice D is the only answer that does this correctly.

35. A: When a series has more than two items, the items should be separated by commas. Choice A is the only one that has commas between the fruits in the series.

36. C: Sometimes you can figure out what a word means by looking at its parts. The word "homophone" includes "phon." This root word is also used in "telephone," "phonograph," and "phonics." What do these words have in common? They all have something to do with sound.

37. D: The phrase "pretty as a picture" is a simile. Similes are descriptions that compare two different things. Comparing a meadow to a pretty picture is a way of saying the meadow looks nice.

38. B: Sometimes you can figure out a word's meaning by using words with the opposite meaning. These are called antonyms. The sentence says, "Tina used to be happy." This means she isn't happy anymore. "Angry" is the opposite of "happy."

39. C: People from different parts of the country speak in different ways. Based on the lines, you can guess that Candace lives in a different part of the country from Bill and Serena. Candace lives in Georgia. Some people in Georgia use the word "y'all" instead of "you all."

40. B: This sentence is about something that is going to happen in the future. The correct way to show the future perfect tense is by using "will have."

41. A: Sometimes a sentence is better if it is shorter. The words "bright" and "light" mean the same thing in this sentence. So there is no need to include both of them. Choice B just switches the words "bright" and light." Choice C is not a complete sentence. Choice D adds another word the sentence does not need, because "shiny" means "bright" and "light."

42. D: A song title should always be placed inside quotation marks.

43. C: The word "similarly" is used to show that two things are the same in some way. Both Pete and Keith play instruments, so they are similar.

44. B: The word "while" shows that both parts of this sentence happen at the same time. The original sentence is wrong because the verb "washing" is written in the present tense, but the verb "walked" is in the past tense. Only choice B has both verbs written in the same tense.

45. D: The phrase "The cat and dog are" shows that this sentence takes place in the present. The present tense version of the verb "sleep" is "sleeping."

46. A: A plant will die if it does not get water. You can use this fact to help you figure out that "perish" means "die."

Online Resources

Due to our efforts to try to keep this book to a manageable length, we've created a link that will give you access to all of your online resources:

mometrix.com/resources719/ssmcag5readwb

It's Your Moment, Let's Celebrate It!

Share your story @mometrixtestpreparation